"Speech Acts" and the First Amendment

Franklyn S. Haiman

With a Foreword by
Abner J. Mikva

Southern Illinois University Press
Carbondale and Edwardsville

Excerpts from "Sticks and Stones Can Put You in Jail, but Can Words
Increase Your Sentence?" by Susan Gellman were originally pub-
lished in 39 UCLA L. Rev. 333, Copyright 1991, The Regents of the
University of California. All Rights Reserved.

Excerpts from "Schools Are Newest Arena for Sex-Harassment
Cases" by Jane Gross are Copyright © 1992 by The New York Times
Company. Reprinted by permission.

Library of Congress Cataloging-in-Publication Data

Haiman, Franklyn Saul.
    "Speech acts" and the First Amendment / Franklyn S.
Haiman ; with a foreword by Abner J. Mikva.
        p. cm.
    Includes index.
    1. Freedom of speech—United States. 2. Libel and slander—
United States. 3. Hate crimes—United States. I. Title.
KF4772.H343 1993
342.73'0953—dc20
[347.302853]   92-21157
ISBN 0-8093-1882-2   CIP

The paper used in this publication meets the minimum requirements
of American National Standard for Information Sciences—Perma-
nence of Paper for Printed Library Materials, ANSI 239.48-1984. ∞

To my sons, Eric and Mark,
whose generation will know whether
the words of this book have any consequences

Contents

Foreword

Franklyn Haiman has a devastating capacity to disrobe the emperor. In the field of First Amendment literature, where lawyers and judges and law teachers weave complicated and gossamer webs to explain often irreconcilable laws and cases, Professor Haiman has frequently punctured the balloons we use to obscure our confusion. He has succeeded remarkably well in his current work.

"Speech acts" is a deliberately vague term used by the legal community to explain why the same judges and politicians who can brag about the First Amendment to our Constitution on the Fourth of July and to foreign visitors are so quick to claim exceptions to the freedom of speech when put to the test. As Professor Haiman explains in his preface, he hopes to delegitimize the term by exposing its ambiguity. He accomplishes that objective very effectively.

The ink could hardly have been dry on the First Amendment before people were beginning to carve out exceptions to it. Perhaps that is so, as Dean Bollinger of the University of Michigan Law School has said, because the First Amendment was never expected to be black-letter law. Rather it is a goal of a free society, which gets nearer or further as our security ebbs and flows. The less secure we are about our country, our happiness, or our self-esteem, the less tolerant we are of strong speech. Dean Bollinger's thesis explains the existence of so many campus codes of conduct that seek to regulate the speech of college students. Professor Haiman devotes a chapter to the problem, showing how unsatisfactory such codes are to solve the problem of hate speech. Since few are secure about the way their own children were raised, let alone other people's children, it is not surprising that there are so many efforts to regulate and restrict the nasty things that college students (and others) can say to each other.

The really provocative analysis in this book relates to the "harm" that speech acts are supposed to cause. We all are ready to concede that no one has ever been raped by a book. We are less likely to concede that no one has been emotionally hurt by hurtful words and deeds. Whether it is the Nazis marching in Skokie or graffiti artists painting racial and religious epithets in various places, we reach for remedies for the scars, even though they are not physical scars. Professor Haiman acknowledges society's urge to "do something" about pornography and nasty words, but he points out the futility of pretending that something other than speech is involved or that we can avoid the price we pay whenever freedom of speech is relegated to lip service.

It is never comfortable to have one's shibboleths exposed. Those who write the literature that seeks to defend restrictions on free speech by resorting to speech-act analysis will not be comforted by this book. I have no doubt that Frank Haiman will be pleased to know that he has once again afflicted the comfortable.

Abner J. Mikva
Chief Judge
United States Court of Appeals
District of Columbia Circuit

Preface

The title of this book is an anti-title. It is designed to call attention to an increasingly popular verbal construct, "speech acts," that I propose to delegitimize.

The human ability to attach labels to phenomena in the real world can be a source of great understanding or of vast confusion. This book will seek to demonstrate that the speech act concept has been the source of more mischief than enlightenment in our discourse about freedom of speech. The problem, as we shall see, is that it means everything or nothing at all. Our thinking about the First Amendment will be enhanced by doing without it.

This volume has grown from seeds that were planted in my 1991 Silha Lecture sponsored by the University of Minnesota's Silha Center for the Study of Media Ethics and Law.

"Speech Acts"
and the
First Amendment

1

Introduction

In February of 1991 a student was expelled from Brown University for shouting racist, anti-Semitic, and homophobic epithets outside of a campus dormitory while in a drunken state. He had been found guilty, apparently for the second time, of violating that school's rules against "showing flagrant disrespect for the well-being of others," engaging in "abusive, threatening or demeaning actions based on race, religion, gender, handicap, ethnicity, national origin, or sexual orientation," and excessive drinking.[1]

In response to criticism that the university's action constituted a curb on freedom of speech, Brown's president, Vartan Gregorian, wrote a letter to the *New York Times*, which was published on 21 February 1991. He claimed that "Brown University has never expelled anyone for free speech, nor will it ever do so." He asserted that the university's code of conduct, under which this student had been expelled, "does not prohibit speech; it prohibits *actions*, and these include behavior that 'shows flagrant disrepect for the well-being of others.' . . . The rules do not proscribe words, epithets, or slanders; they proscribe behavior." Gregorian then addressed the particulars of the event at hand. "The point at which speech becomes behavior and the degree to which that behavior shows flagrant disrespect for the well-being of others (Offense II), subjects someone to abusive or demeaning actions (Offense III) or is related to drug or alcohol abuse (Offense IV) is determined by a hearing to consider the circumstances of each case."[2]

President Gregorian was not the first, nor will he be the last, either to confuse speech with action, or to blur the line between them, or to believe and assert that, under some circumstances, speech *becomes* action. Indeed, one of the most frequent justifications offered for limitations on freedom of speech, whether in scholarly or popular discourse about the First Amendment, is that certain types of speech are really speech acts and should therefore be treated differently from "pure" speech, that is, subjected to the same scrutiny and possible regulation by society as other kinds of regulable action, behavior, or conduct. Even such prominent First Amendment scholars as Thomas Emerson and Frederick Schauer have held that *only* by classifying certain types of harmful speech as action, and thus outside the parameters of freedom of speech, can we preserve the undiluted strength of First Amendment protection for speech that truly merits the special insulation from social control that the First Amendment was designed to provide.[3]

However, Schauer parts company from Emerson in believing that Emerson's introduction into First Amendment discourse of the phrase *freedom of expression* as a substitute for the more traditional *freedom of speech* was unfortunate. In Schauer's view, the substitution invited for possible inclusion under First Amendment protection a variety of nonverbal acts that more properly belong outside the highly exclusive domain governed by the free speech principle.[4] That inclusion, indeed, was one of Emerson's goals.

Still another scholar, Stanley Fish, has succinctly explained why the distinction relied upon by Emerson and Schauer between speech and action is "essential to First Amendment jurisprudence."

> No one would think to frame a First Amendment that began "Congress shall make no law abridging freedom of action"; for that would amount to saying "Congress shall make no law," which would amount to saying "There shall be no law." . . . If the First Amendment is to make any sense, have any bite, speech must be declared not to be a species of action, or to be a special form of action lacking the aspects of action that cause it to be the object of regulation.[5]

Examples of moves to carve exceptions out of the First Amendment by defining certain kinds of speech as action are numerous and did not begin with the controversy of recent years over whether there should be college rules, state legislation, or court decisions excluding racist, sexist, and homophobic verbal abuse from the arena of protected speech. As long ago as 1942, the Supreme Court gave its approval to what it called the "fighting words" doctrine, denying First Amendment protection to words "which by their very utterance inflict injury or tend to incite an immediate breach of the peace."[6] Although the Supreme Court did not itself do so, many contemporary defenders of the fighting words doctrine describe such words as speech acts, analogous to knocking a chip off somebody's shoulder, rather than the communication of ideas, which the authors of the First Amendment had in mind. The Supreme Court's own language in explaining why fighting words, as well as obscenity and libel, are not protected by the First Amendment was that they "are no essential part of any exposition of ideas, and are of such slight social value as a step to truth that any benefit that may be derived from them is clearly outweighed by the social interests in order and morality."[7] Thus, it would seem that the Court, rather than regarding fighting words as speech acts, saw them as verbalisms pure and simple, but verbalisms of such "slight social value" that they were not "essential" to the "exposition" of the speaker's point of view. I will return to this argument later.

Obscene material, as just noted, is another category of communication that the Supreme Court has placed beyond the umbrella of First Amendment protection and that has since been regarded by some writers and legal scholars as a speech act rather than pure speech. According to an early version of this point of view, the reading of obscene books or magazines and the viewing of obscene pictures, movies, or live performances was essentially the same as masturbating or fondling a simulated sex organ and was thus allegedly a response to a physical stimulus rather than to the expression of ideas.[8]

In a more recent version of the speech-act perspective on obscenity, some feminist scholars have argued that pornographic pictures that portray women in demeaning ways or as the victims of sexual violence are *acts* of subordination that reinforce and perpetuate the male dominance that exists in our society.[9] As one law review article has described this point of view, "pornography is not expression depicting the subordination of women but is the practice of subordination itself."[10]

By the same line of reasoning, some who advocate restricting racist epithets and other verbal abuse of groups that have routinely suffered discrimination claim that such expression "is particularly harmful because it is a mechanism of subordination, reinforcing a historical vertical relationship."[11] Viewed as a mechanism of subordination it is, thus, allegedly a speech act rather than mere speech.

But perhaps the most sophisticated and complicated example of proposed exceptions to the First Amendment based on the speech-act concept is the work of Kent Greenawalt in his 1989 book *Speech, Crime, and the Uses of Language*. His ideas, examined in more detail in the next chapter, are based on the premise that particular kinds of speech, such as the giving of orders or the making of manipulative threats, go beyond the mere assertion of facts or values to become "situation-altering utterances." As such, he maintains, they "are ways of doing things, not asserting things" and are thus "subject to regulation on the same bases as most noncommunicative behavior" that is "outside the scope of a principle of free speech."[12]

What all of these examples have in common is a bit of word magic whereby the flapping of vocal chords, the scratching of a pen, the display of a picture, or the hoisting of a banner are transformed from symbolic to nonsymbolic behavior by an act of definition. To be sure, all symbolic behavior, whether it be a public speech, a newspaper editorial, a movie, or the waving of a flag, has its physical elements. First Amendment scholar Harry Kalven, Jr., noted long ago that "all speech is necessarily 'speech plus.' If it is oral, it is noise and may interrupt someone else; if it is written, it may be litter."[13] I would add that a protest march in the streets invariably detours traffic and a banner may block somebody's view of something he or she wants to see.

But the elements of symbolic behavior that the proponents of the speech-act concept would restrict are *not* those incidental physical by-products of communicative behavior. Those effects are governable, if necessary, by content-neutral rules of time and place, which no reasonable defender of First Amendment rights disputes. What speech-act theorists *would* restrict are the symbolic elements themselves—the ideas and meanings contained in the words, pictures, or representations in question—for it is these elements, or more accurately their consequences, that create the problems they seek to address. The proof of this claim is that if these ideas or meanings were expressed in a foreign language unknown to their audience, clothed in unfamiliar symbols, or portrayed by incomprehensible images, there would be no harmful consequences about which to be concerned. Indeed, there would be no consequences at all.

What has converted speech into a speech act for those who choose to define it that way—be it fighting words, obscenity, racist slurs, orders, or threats—are the ideas or meanings that have been communicated to persons who understand them. One can call it an *act* if one wishes to—as Humpty Dumpty in *Through the Looking Glass* observed, you can name anything whatever you want to—but it is still essentially a *symbolic*, not a *physical*, transaction. And though it is true that symbols can, and commonly do, arouse physiological as well as mental responses in their audience, the mental response comes first and mediates what follows. Without a response of the mind, nothing follows, for nothing has been comprehended.

Thus, the thesis of this book is that a fundamental difference obtains between symbolic and nonsymbolic interactions and that the First Amendment is *always* implicated in the former and only occasionally in the latter. I do not claim that because freedom of speech is implicated it will necessarily prevail over all other possible competing interests. Some symbolic behavior may be so harmful that we are justified in restraining it, but not because a court or legal theorist has labeled it a speech act entirely beyond the purview of the First Amendment.

If it is true that all symbolic behaviors have physical by-products that can legitimately be regulated in a fair and neutral way,[14] is it not also true that all nonsymbolic behaviors contain symbolic elements that might conceivably lay claim to First Amendment protection? Thus, a presidential assassin might plead that he or she acted for the purpose of sending a political message to the public, and a group of vandals who burned a cross on the lawn of an African American family or defaced the wall of a Jewish temple with swastikas might make the same claim. And, indeed, communication to the world at large might very well have been their primary motivation. Does that make their behavior a speech act?

To regard such claims as legitimate again blurs the line we must maintain between speech and action—between symbolism and the reality it may represent—if the First Amendment is to make any sense. Burning the president in effigy is symbolic behavior (with the physical by-product of a pile of ashes) that qualifies as speech. Killing the president (with the symbolic by-product of sending a political message to the world) has palpable physical consequences that cannot be tolerated in a law-abiding society. Burning a cross on one's own lawn or displaying a swastika at a rally in a public park is symbolic behavior that qualifies as speech. Burning a cross on somebody else's lawn, putting a torch to his or her house, painting a swastika on a group's place of worship or breaking their windows are acts of physical trespass and defacement or destruction of property that are legally punishable, regardless of their possible symbolic purposes or effects.

What about the public burning of one's draft card at an antiwar rally or sleeping in tents in the park across from the White House to dramatize the plight of the homeless? Are these speech acts deserving consideration as possible candidates for First Amendment protection? Acts they certainly are, with palpable physical consequences—in the former case, destroying a certificate issued by the government as a means of identifying draft registrants, and in the latter, potentially tearing up the turf or requiring all-night policing. That these are arguably victimless acts undertaken for the sole or primary purpose of communicating a political message to the world raises interesting and serious First Amendment questions that are not raised by assassinations, arson, or trespass. I will turn to an analysis of those questions later, but not because a court or legal theorist has decided to anoint them with the label of speech acts, a category that, if accepted as a conceptual framework, would necessarily also encompass most assassinations and many acts of arson and trespass.

I have already noted why it is necessary to distinguish speech from action if the First Amendment is to have any meaning other than the senseless proposition that the government shall make no laws. What I have not yet done is explain why it matters that the First Amendment's special protection for freedom of speech be kept as undiluted as possible. The values to a society of a strong guarantee of freedom of speech have long been the subject of discussion by political philosophers and legal scholars, to the point where we have accumulated a host of reasons why it is important that we have a First Amendment. Only with great humility can one presume to add anything useful to that discussion, but like many others in recent years, I believe it helpful. I do so not because I share the view of some that the traditional justifications are fundamentally flawed, though I concur with the criticism that the marketplace of ideas concept, for one, has been overplayed and underexamined. Nor do I wish, as some have done, to suggest that the value I find most significant should be substituted for the others. I have never understood why freedom of speech must be justified by only one overarching value. What I intend is to propose an additional reason for valuing the First Amendment, based on my understanding of the nature of symbolic processes.

First let us briefly review the already rich roster of justifications for freedom of speech to which I am offering a modest postscript. Thomas Emerson's classic work *The System of Freedom of Expression* summarized four values that that system serves.[15] Borrowing from the political philosopher Alexander Meiklejohn,[16] he identified the first value as the participation in self-government that freedom of speech makes possible and without which it cannot happen.

From John Stuart Mill's famous essay *On Liberty* and the writings of many others came a second value, that a free and unfettered marketplace of ideas is the best way to conduct a search for truth—not because truth will always prevail over falsehood, as John Milton alleged in his famous *Areopagitica*, and as many critics who misunderstand the theory enjoy pointing out, but because there is ordinarily a better chance of approximating the truth when ideas are challenged by competing ideas than when they are dogmatically asserted and accepted.

Emerson's third value is self-expression, the healthful opportunity the First Amendment provides for individuals to say what is on their minds and to express their creativity through literature, science, art, music, and so on. This value is not essentially different from the "self-realization" concept Martin Redish later advanced as the core value of the First Amendment or the "human liberty" justification C. Edwin Baker propounded.[17]

The fourth value Emerson identified is catharsis and the consequent maintenance of a balance in society between stability and change. By letting people blow off steam, a society not only preserves its equilibrium in the short run, but is made aware of problems that need to be addressed if that stability is to be sustained in the long run.

Although Emerson's fourfold inventory has served as the most common reference point for those who have since written about the purposes of the First Amendment, it neither exhausted the field already plowed nor anticipated more proposed values that were to come later. As to the past, Emerson overlooked another of John Stuart Mill's significant insights, that even truth, if it goes unquestioned, becomes mere prejudice, with people forgetting the reasons for their beliefs and newer generations perhaps never learning them. Like unused muscles that grow flabby, unchallenged minds become atrophied.

Since Emerson wrote in 1970 a stream of scholarly books and articles have added to his catalog or proposed substitutes for items in it. Vincent Blasi wrote in 1977 about the "checking value" of the First Amendment,[18] which journalists have long regarded as the watchdog function of the press vis-à-vis the operations of the government. Frederick Schauer, writing in 1982 and explaining his dissatisfaction with traditional justifications for the First Amendment, concluded that "the most persuasive argument for a Free Speech Principle is what may be characterized as government incompetence," the inability of fallible political leaders, if they exercise censorship powers, to make trustworthy distinctions between truth and falsity.[19] Lee Bollinger, in 1986, offered the thesis that even if a free marketplace produces horrendous ideas, practicing tolerance for them contributes to the health and strength of a society and its members.[20] Paul Chevigny followed, in 1987, with the view that dialogue is the essence of democracy, and Steven Shiffrin, in 1990, with an emphasis on the role and value of dissenters in a free society[21]— both of which can be interpreted as more sophisticated and contemporary elaborations of what John Stuart Mill said back in 1859.

My own contribution to the list may have little claim to originality, since it is perhaps already implicit in the self-realization value that has been so widely, though not universally, accepted as one of the purposes of the First Amendment. I have already asserted that symbolic and nonsymbolic transactions are fundamentally different processes. I would now add that the ability to use, transmit, comprehend, and respond to symbols is a uniquely human capacity setting us apart from all other earthly creatures. Although there are indications that chimpanzees, dolphins, and whales can learn to manipulate and respond to simple symbols and that dogs may dream, none of them have written history books nor told stories to their offspring that would enable those later generations to learn from the mistakes of their predecessors. Nor have they put paintings on cave walls. It often has been argued that the most defining characteristic of what it means to be human is this symbol-creating and symbol-transmitting capability. And if that is what being human is mainly about, what could be more important than a First Amendment that protects and nurtures it?

2

Situation-Altering
Utterances

One field of scholarly endeavor that has grown substantially during the past half century is linguistics and the philosophy of language. And perhaps no other contribution from that area has had more widespread influence than speech act theory, succinctly summarized by one of the field's early leaders, Ludwig Wittgenstein, in the assertion that "words are deeds."[1]

From that simple premise has flowed an outpouring of literature identifying, describing, and classifying the many different ways in which words are said to be deeds. J. L. Austin and John R. Searle have piloted the way with leading books and essays on such verbalisms.[2] Whether labeling them "performative utterances" or "illocutionary acts," they distinguish these uses of language from "locutions"—statements that only assert facts or values—on the ground that their mere utterance brings about some new state of affairs. Favorite examples are marriage vows that bind a couple into a new relationship and a general's commands that send troops into battle.

Most linguists and philosophers of language who have dealt with speech act theory have said little about the implications of their work for freedom of speech and the First Amendment.[3] That concern was largely left to law professor Kent Greenawalt, who adopted the theory to explain and justify the multitude of exceptions to the First Amendment found in tort and criminal law.[4] Greenawalt's categories of speech that do not qualify for First Amendment protection are all built on the common premise that they "are ways of doing things, not of asserting things" and are thus "subject to regulation on the same bases as most noncommunicative behavior" that is "outside the scope of a principle of free speech."[5] He coins the phrase "situation-altering utterances," which he prefers to what he regards as the broader and more ambiguous concepts of performative or illocutionary statements, and which he defines as utterances that are "a means for changing the social context in which we live."[6]

Let us examine some of Greenawalt's categories, based largely on those identified by Austin and Searle, to determine how sound his analysis is. He claims that certain promises and agreements—such as the utterance of marriage vows, or the making of a contract (either oral or written), or an announcement of the results of a vote—alter the world by creating obligations that did not exist before.[7] One probably must grant his premise that the expression of these words creates obligations *in the participants' minds* that did not exist before and that in a psychological and even legal sense the situation has therefore been altered. But whether that alteration will ever mean anything depends on how the parties actually behave *after* the words have been uttered. Do the spouses actually love and honor one another until death does them part? Do the contracting parties deliver on their part of the deal, and do the voters conform their conduct to what the majority has agreed to? To put it another way, the words that were uttered accomplish nothing unless they are taken seriously and there are other forces at work beyond the words themselves to make them stick, such as continuing benefits to be gained from the agreement, possible feelings of guilt over noncompliance, or even the possibility of legal enforcement of the contract.

Conversely, we know very well that two individuals can live together in love and mutual respect without ever uttering any marriage vows, that people can engage in mutually beneficial trades without any prior formal written or oral agreement, and that the members of a group can conform their behavior to the norms of that group without any laws having been passed or explicit rules promulgated. What altered *their* situation from what it may have been before? I would suggest that whatever mutual interest brought it about and sustains it is the same as that which brought about and sustains the situation of those who have made verbal commitments and that in both instances an erosion of that mutual interest will lead to a de facto break in the relationship whether or not verbal promises and agreements have been made. In short, the utterance of marriage vows, the signing of a contract, or the announcement of the results of a vote are simply rituals announcing a reality that is already ripe for enactment rather than instruments for bringing about that reality. Whether or not anything different actually happens pursuant to the utterance will not be primarily a consequence of the words spoken but of what the parties choose to do or not to do for other reasons. To say this is not to deny that the verbal commitment may add some psychological pressure to perform as agreed, but again, that would be due not to the words themselves but to one's anticipation of the other party's possible reaction to a welching on the promise. Nor do I deny that the words spoken or written may make legal enforcment of the agreement possible where it would not be possible in their absence and that it is a significant alteration of the situation if, in fact, legal processes are ever invoked. But whether those processes are invoked or not, and whether or not they succeed in enforcing the agreement, depends on a variety of factors beyond the words of the agreement themselves. The words alone, without human agents who are persuaded, for whatever reasons, to act upon them, change nothing. It is, therefore, difficult for me to see how they qualify as "deeds."

I am not saying that promises and agreements mean nothing or that they should not be honored or even, under appropriate circumstances, be enforced by the law. I believe that speech is important, which is why I care as much as I do about the First Amendment. But the importance and power of speech lies in its ability to persuade, not in its ability to enact. It commonly precedes deeds, it often confirms their existence and facilitates their enactment, and it sometimes announces their demise. But it is not per se a deed.

I turn now to Greenawalt's category of orders, permissions, and other verbal exercises of official authority. Some examples are the umpire calling, "You're out," the teacher excusing a student to go to the restroom, the boss telling you, "You're fired," or the general ordering troops into battle. These are the kinds of statements that Greenawalt says change the world by creating duties or rights to perform or not to perform in particular ways and are thus speech acts rather than pure speech.[8]

But is it the umpire's words that cause the batter to go back to the dugout after his third strike or is it the player's third strike itself, plus a preexisting understanding that a batter is only allowed three strikes in the game of baseball and that the umpire is the one in whom authority has been vested to confirm when that has happened? If someone in the grandstand had shouted out those same words, the batter could justifiably ignore them. It is the official position of the umpire, not the words themselves, to which the batter defers.

The same authority of position is true of the boss and the general. You can, if you wish, ignore the words of the boss saying you are fired and consider yourself still employed. The only problems are that you will not receive any more paychecks and you may be physically ejected from the premises. But unless and until those physical acts occur, you are not, in fact, fired unless you voluntarily accept your employer's verbal definition of the situation. If you do not, the employer's words have enacted nothing. That boss will have to back them up with the measures just noted for them to have any effect.

Similarly, in the case of a general's orders, soldiers can, and sometimes do, disobey. They may be shot as a result, and that will certainly alter their situation. But until that happens or they are caught and sent to prison or dishonorably discharged from the service, the words of the order to advance have produced no effects. To be sure, as with the signing of a contract, that order may provide a legal basis for imprisoning or shooting the wayward soldier, but that order is again only an authorization for an action, not the action itself.

What about the soldiers who obey the general's order? Has not the commander's utterance been a speech act for them? It has not, any more than it has for the soldier who disobeyed. Like the batter who has struck out, the soldiers follow the general's directive because they believe in the war they are fighting (as the batter believes in the game of baseball) or because they accept the authority of the state and are unwilling to become conscientious objectors. As one commentator on military authority has put it, "Discipline and morale influence the inarticulate vote that is instantaneously taken by masses of men when the order comes to move forward. . . . [T]he Army does not move forward until the motion has 'carried.'"[9] That may be taking a bit of poetic license in describing what has happened, but the underlying point is valid nonetheless.

The teacher giving a student permission to go to the restroom is another example of someone whose official position gives him or her the authority to control the movements of others. The fact that words are used in the exercise of that authority does not endow the words themselves with any force. The force comes from the teacher's ability to punish students for ignoring those words, *if* the teacher so chooses and *if* the student fears that punishment. If the student's need to go to the restroom is sufficiently urgent and the likelihood of serious punishment sufficiently remote, the teacher's denial of permission will likely be ignored. In other words, the speech of the teacher will have no effect. If the teacher's granting of permission is pro forma, occurring whenever a student asks to leave the room, that speech likewise has no significant effect. It is a mere ritual that acknowledges the teacher's position of authority without substantially influencing the particular behavior of going to the restroom. Students would leave whether or not the words were uttered.

Even Austin and Searle, the leading champions of speech act theory, seem to recognize, without admitting it, that the utterances they allege to be doing something rather than saying something are not really doing all they claim. One example Austin gives of a performative utterance is christening a ship. Presumably, the ceremony of naming a ship the *Queen Elizabeth* while smashing a champagne bottle against it accomplishes the deed. Yet Austin notes that if "some low type comes up, snatches the bottle out of your hand, breaks it on the stem, shouts out 'I name this ship the *Generalissimo Stalin*' and then for good measure kicks away the chocks,"[10] the ship will not actually have been named *Generalissimo Stalin*.

Why not? Although Austin does not explain it, the primary reason is that nobody is going to paint that name on the hull or use it to refer to the ship in the future. But it would also be true of the name *Queen Elizabeth* if the christening ceremony were not accompanied by the painting of *that* name on the hull and if *that* name were not used afterward on advertising brochures, on tickets, and in other references to the vessel. That it was a "lowly type" who preferred to call it *Generalissimo Stalin* and a recognized celebrity who uttered the words *Queen Elizabeth* is one relevant factor in determining the consequences of their respective statements, but not the only one.

Searle explicitly acknowledges that "there are a large number of illocutionary acts that require an extra-linguistic institution, and generally a special position by the speaker and hearer within that institution in order for the act to be performed," but he denies that all illocutionary acts are dependent on position or any other kind of extralinguistic force.[11] He illustrates those words that do depend on extralinguistic elements by referring to utterances of blessing or excommunication, which are only enactments if emanating from someone in the position of priest in a church. On the other hand, he suggests that a statement such as "I classify this as an A and this as a B" is a done deed.[12] But I would argue that this event is no different than naming a ship the *Queen Elizabeth*. Labels and names are enactments only if they are *used*, by the one bestowing the label or by others, as a basis for sorting things out, finding an object, pointing others to it, and so on. Although it is true that the repeated use of a name is itself purely a speech behavior that appears, superficially, to be a kind of enactment, it is only an enactment in the sense that everyone has accepted and internalized that usage and behaves accordingly. If nobody paid any attention to the definitions of words that are given in a dictionary and, as Humpty Dumpty suggested, used them in any random way they chose, the authors of the dictionary would have enacted nothing.

The last of Greenawalt's categories I will address is what he calls "manipulative inducements" or threats, such as "Do this and I'll increase my business with you" and "Don't do that or I'll hit you." Such statements, says Greenawalt, are not merely the communication of information about what may happen in the future, but are critical elements in bringing about that future and thus are situation-altering.[13] He tries, unsuccessfully I think, to distinguish these utterances from those in which people sincerely state what they intend to, and will in fact, do in the future if the person to whom they are speaking engages in certain behavior; that is, statements not intended to manipulate the other person, but merely to provide information as to what the consequences of certain events are likely to be.

But how can someone tell which type of statement it is when one says to a spouse, "Unless you stop drinking, I'm going to have to leave you"? Would that speaker even know for sure how sincere the prediction is, whether it would ever be enacted, and whether it is manipulation, persuasion, or merely a statement of fact? If classifying it as a situation-altering utterance or speech act depends on answering those questions, it would seem to be a fruitless enterprise. Why not, instead, view it simply as speech that will or will not change the addressee's behavior (if that was even its purpose), depending on a host of variables, some of which may be responsive to the thoughts and feelings expressed in the statement, and others that may be entirely irrelevant to it.

Speech act theory becomes most plausible, whether in Greenawalt's discussion or that of others, when the utterances being considered contain direct threats of physical or material harm. Intimidating statements of that kind are said to be situation-altering speech acts because they leave their victims with no choice of what to do; they are coercive, not persuasive. But what does it really mean to say that speech is coercive? How can words by themselves make anybody do anything he or she does not want to do? The answer is they cannot. What they can do is vividly describe for their audience the consequences that will befall them if they fail to abide by the speaker's wishes. The audience then has a choice. They can conform and hopefully avoid that fate, or they can refuse to conform and take the consequences. If those consequences are death or disaster for themselves or for others they care about, it is not much of a choice. But it is a choice, nonetheless, and the instances are many in human history when women and men have chosen death over surrender.

It should be noted, however, that sometimes the threatened consequences do not occur even if the communicator's demands are rejected, perhaps because of a lack of will or means to carry out the threat or because changed circumstances make it unwise or physically impossible. So again we see that there is time and space between speech and action—sometimes only a moment and sometimes more, sometimes an inch and sometimes a continent—but there is always the opportunity for the audience to think about what has been said and decide what to do about it, and always the chance that what has been threatened may not ensue.

The point is not that direct threats and intimidation are benign and should not, under certain circumstances, be against the law. I think they should be. There may be differences of opinion as to how explicit and direct threats must be, and how immediate the possible consequences of noncompliance, for them to be considered legally punishable, but at some point the choices they leave to the victims are so unacceptable, and the possible consequences of rejection so destructive, that no one would dispute the validity of prohibiting them.[14] But that assessment cannot be made out of context or by a theorist's a priori decision to classify *all* threatening utterances as speech acts that are categorically beyond the protection of the First Amendment.

A threat by a 125-pound weakling to punch out a 250-pound football player is not the same as the threat of a teenage gang with a history of violence to beat up or kill anyone who enters their turf. Some people feel intimidated by a nasty look or mildly critical comments; others would not budge if a bulldozer were about to plow into them. A holdup with an unloaded or toy gun will be effective if the victim believes the gun to be real and loaded, but if somehow the victim realizes that it is a toy or is not loaded, the stickup will fail.

In short, the decision whether a credibly threatening message has been sent *and* received can only be made by evaluating the specific circumstances of a particular interaction. Indeed, this is true of *any* symbolic transaction. Its meaning and significance can only be understood by taking into account not only the symbolic stimulus, but the mental response of its audience, the relationship of the parties involved, and the context in which it occurs. If that is done, and it is found that a victim has in fact been intimidated by an utterance that any normal person might reasonably perceive as menacing, it would then be appropriate to invoke legal remedies against the pure speech in question.

This idea is by no means original. It is the way the law usually works presently with respect to threatening verbal utterances. However, current law enforcement sometimes goes astray when judges attracted to speech act theory apply it to instances of nonverbal, but symbolic, behavior because certain physical by-products or components lead them to believe that more than speech is involved. The Supreme Court, in its ruling in *U.S. v. O'Brien*, the famous draft card burning case, unfortunately opened the door for judges to make this mistake. In that case, which did involve more than just symbolic behavior, the Court declared:

> We cannot accept the view that an apparently limitless variety of conduct can be labelled "speech" whenever the person engaging in the conduct intends thereby to express an idea. . . . [W]hen "speech" and "nonspeech" elements are combined in the same course of conduct, a sufficiently important government interest in regulating the nonspeech element can justify incidental limitations

on First Amendment freedoms. . . . [W]e think it is clear that a government regulation is sufficiently justified if it is within the constitutional power of government; if it furthers an important or substantial government interest; if the governmental interest is unrelated to the suppression of free expression; and if the incidental restriction on alleged First Amendment freedom is no greater than is essential to the furtherance of that interest.[15]

I have no quarrel with these standards when used to deal with cases like draft card burning or camping in a park, where the conduct in question has significant physical consequences that are ordinarily and legitimately subject to social control. As I explain in a later chapter, I do not agree with the Supreme Court's conclusion that punishing O'Brien for burning his draft card met the standards that the Court itself established in that case, and I am ambivalent about the way the majority applied those standards with respect to sleeping in Lafayette Park, but the criteria themselves make sense in those contexts.

What does not make sense to me is the use of the O'Brien standards in cases where the conduct, though nonverbal, is essentially symbolic and where the same First Amendment tests that are used in cases of verbal communication should apply. Thus, it has been inappropriate for the courts to use the O'Brien criteria with respect to burning one's own flag, which is as much speech and as little action as an oration or an editorial verbally condemning the flag.

A dramatic example of what goes wrong when a court applies the O'Brien tests to symbolic behavior is the 1990 decision of the U.S. Second Circuit Court of Appeals that a New York City Transit Authority's ban on begging or panhandling in subway stations did not violate the First Amendment. The district court judge who initially heard the case had decided that it did[16] and was overruled by the appellate court.[17] The two-person majority of the Second Circuit panel that decided the case started its argument on the wrong foot with the premise that "common sense tells us that begging is much more 'conduct' than it is 'speech.'"[18] I would suggest that common sense should tell us just the opposite. Since when is talking to someone, whether asking for money or which train to take, not speech?

What actually bothered the two judges is revealed when they explain why it was permissible for the transit authority to prohibit panhandling, but not charitable solicitations. "While organized charities serve community interests by enhancing communication and disseminating ideas, the conduct of begging and panhandling in the subway amounts to nothing less than a menace to the common good."[19] To this explanation, the panel's third member, dissenting in part, observed, "the difficult question for me is whether any legally justifiable distinction can be drawn between begging for one's self and solicitation for organized charities. I am unable to do so, and therefore I respectfully dissent."[20]

In other words, the majority found the prohibition against panhandling acceptable not, as they claimed, because begging is conduct, but because it is, in their view, speech of lesser social value than asking for money for a charity. Their own justification for distinguishing between panhandling and charitable solicitations belies their later assertion that "like O'Brien, the case now at bar involves proscription of conduct for reasons completely unrelated to the alleged communicative impact of the conduct."[21]

Let me make clear that I am not arguing that the First Amendment would necessarily prohibit a transit authority decision that banned all approaches of closer than one foot to strangers in subway stations to say anything at all to them. Hypothetically, although improbably, that might be justified because those places had become so dangerous, and such physical approaches so intimidating, that a state of virtual martial law would be required. Nor am I claiming that the First Amendment would necessarily prohibit the banning of *all* solicitations for money in subway stations (presumably including the seeking of change for a soft drink machine). The first would be a content-neutral regulation of a physical by-product of speech, and the second a time and place limit on speech itself, both *perhaps* justified by the extraordinary circumstances in a subway station with respect to danger and potential violence. But to tell only those who are dirty or poorly dressed (i.e., symbolically unsavory) that they cannot approach and talk to strangers, or to tell it only to those who seek charity for themselves rather than for others, is to have a government policy that the First Amendment should forbid.

The judges who upheld the ban on panhandling may have been motivated in part by another premise they did not articulate in their opinion—namely, that physical approaches to people can, in some circumstances, be as intimidating as directly threatening words and prohibitable on the same basis. That appears to be the rationale for the occasional police or court orders that require protesters outside an abortion clinic to keep a specified distance from the building's entrance, a distance that is greater than necessary simply to insure physical access to the clinic. To my knowledge, such limits have not been imposed on labor picketers, although their close physical proximity to customers or scabs who cross their picket line might be just as intimidating. Whether either, both, or neither of these settings justify such limits is a question of balancing First Amendment rights against competing social interests that might well take precedence over them, a judgment we must trust to our courts. I would urge, however, that in making that decision, judges should understand that mere nonobstructive physical presence, even when enhanced by the shouting of verbal epithets, is symbolic behavior entitled to the strictest First Amendment scrutiny, rather than some kind of speech act that is, per se, situation-altering. Such behavior is per se no different from the epithets themselves which, like promises, agreements, orders, and permissions, are not *by virtue of their mere utterance* situation-altering.

3

Fighting Words
and Incitement

Although most linguists and philosophers of language who have worked in the vineyards of speech act theory have themselves said relatively little about its implications for communication law, others have not been so reticent. As indicated in chapter 1, the notion that verbal utterances sometimes constitute a speech act has been invoked by defenders of the legal doctrine of fighting words to justify the exclusion of such speech from the First Amendment arena. They argue that because fighting words are actually the same as the proverbial knocking of a chip off somebody's shoulder, such words are not really speech in the sense envisioned by the First Amendment and therefore are not protected by it. Provoking a listener into a fight with the speaker, they say, is not an invitation to dialogue, which is what the philosophy of freedom of speech is supposed to be concerned with.[1]

The same line of reasoning has been used, although much less commonly, with regard to utterances that incite sympathetic listeners to engage in violence or in other illegal actions advocated by the speaker—to riot, to burn, to lynch, or to resist military service, for example. Again, these kinds of words are perceived by some to be more than mere speech because of their intimate connection to antisocial action.

With respect to both utterances that are alleged to be fighting words and those that are thought to be incitements to illegal action, the Supreme Court has drawn a boundary line between what is protected by the First Amendment and what is not. In 1969 the Court said of the sympathetic audience situation that the government may not "forbid or proscribe advocacy of the use of force or of law violation except where such advocacy is directed to inciting or producing imminent lawless action and is likely to incite or produce such action."[2] Of the hostile audience context it said, in 1972, that utterances are punishable as fighting words only if "they have a direct tendency to cause acts of violence by the person to whom, individually, the remark is addressed."[3] These two principles are essentially the same in concept; that is, for these kinds of utterances to lose First Amendment protection, there must be a direct relationship between the speech in question and the likelihood of immediate violence or other illegal behavior.

It is significant that both of these precedents were major departures from earlier court rulings on provocative, and inciting, speech. The first time the Court defined fighting words, in 1942, there were two branches to the definition. Fighting words, as discussed in chapter 1, were *either* those that "by their very utterance inflict injury" *or* those that "tend to incite an immediate breach of the peace." But the first of these branches was cut off by the Court in its 1972 ruling, leaving only provocations to physical reactions as punishable speech.

As for the advocacy of illegal action to sympathetic audiences, the Court's decisions from 1919 to 1961, though supposedly following the "clear and present danger" doctrine enunciated in 1919,[4] actually upheld convictions for speech that had only indirect and remote connections to potential illegal action.[5] As late as 1957 and 1961, the Court, while distinguishing between the advocacy of abstract doctrines, which was to be absolutely protected, and the advocacy of illegal action, which was not, explicitly allowed for punishing the advocacy of illegal action whether that action was to be taken "now *or in the future*" (italics mine).[6] Not until 1969 was the more spech-protective requirement that the potential danger be *immediate* added to the mix.

In none of these decisions did the Supreme Court say that the kinds of utterances they were judging were anything other than pure speech, only that the speech was so dangerous or so harmful that society had the right to curb it despite the First Amendment's seemingly absolute prohibition against such limitations.[7] The only hint of what might be considered speech-act thinking (though it preceded the academic development and dissemination of that theory by many years) is suggested implicitly in the now-discarded first branch of the original definition of fighting words, where the Court asserted that words can, *by their very utterance*, inflict injury. In that phrase the justices must have been referring to the psychological injury felt by the target of

abusive language, whether or not those hurt feelings lead the
individual to fight. By dropping that component of the fighting
words doctrine three decades later, the Court seemed to be sig-
naling that it no longer considered such psychological injury
sufficient justification for curbing First Amendment rights.

Regardless of where one draws the line, for First Amendment purposes, between provocative or inciting speech and en-
suing antisocial behavior, there is still *some* time and space between the speech and the action that follows, time and space for
the audience to absorb the speaker's message and decide (though
it may be a split-second decision) what to do about it. As with
the kinds of speech discussed in the previous chapter, any action
that ensues is mediated by the mental processes of the audience.

These processes, unfortunatley, too often appear not to be
understood by judges and legal scholars when they deal with
potentially explosive speech situations where serious dangers to
society are perceived. Judge Learned Hand, in a famous free
speech case arising out of World War I, was one of the earliest
commentators to oversimplify the complexity of the communication process when he wrote that "words are not only the keys of
persuasion, but the triggers of action."[8] He was thus suggesting
that sometimes audiences are like guns that, once their triggers
are pulled, respond automatically and inevitably. This idea
falsely presumes that human beings, like guns, are inanimate
objects that have no consciousness, make no decisions, and react
mechanically to stimuli.[9]

Ironically, Judge Hand, who at that time was a federal district court judge in New York before being promoted to the
Circuit Court of Appeals, used his key and trigger metaphors to
vindicate, rather than suppress, the free speech rights of the
Masses Publishing Company in his finding that its antiwar articles and cartoons were "keys of persuasion" rather than "triggers
of action." But he was overruled by the Court of Appeals, which
held that even such persuasion was too hazardous to be tolerated.[10]

The metaphors that judges (not to mention the rest of us)
use to describe phenomena provide interesting insights into how
they see the world. Moreover, those metaphors significantly
influence their thinking and decision-making.[11] A dramatic example is the frequency with which the metaphor of *fire* has been
employed in free speech court opinions.[12] Dangerous speech

has been depicted as "falsely shouting fire in a theatre,"[13] and compared to a "single revolutionary spark" that "may kindle a fire," which "smoldering for a time, may burst into a sweeping and destructive conflagration."[14] It has also been labeled as hazardous because of the "inflammable nature of world conditions."[15] Leaflets have been likened to "a little breath" that "is enough to kindle a flame,"[16] and as "growing more inflammatory" the farther they are circulated.[17]

If one assumes that speech is like a match or a spark or a small fire that can burst into a bigger one, one commits the same mistake that is made when one presumes that speech is like the trigger of a gun. Fires come into being through a physical chain reaction, without mediation by a human mind or intervention by a human will. The problem with a speech-act perspective, whether explicitly based on contemporary linguistic theories or unconsciously employing metaphors like triggers and fire, is that human beings get left out of the equation.

At this point a reader might be thinking, Wait a minute. Don't people sometimes act like robots? Is the author not giving them too much credit for rational decision-making? But the reader should note that I have claimed nothing about people making *rational* decisions, only that they are *conscious* of what they are doing and, presumably, have the capacity to stop themselves from doing it, no matter how much anger a speaker may have awakened in them. My use of the term *awakened* is itself perhaps as unfortunate a metaphor as triggers and fire, because anger is not literally awakened by words alone. Those words must be followed by the listener's interpretation of their meaning, along with some preexisting hostility or other reason for a readiness to respond violently, plus the physical circumstances that make such a response feasible. Except for the noise they make, words are not like the sound of an alarm clock nor are they comparable to the shaking of someone to wake them up, where the awakening can be immediate and automatic.

To be sure, having the capacity to stop oneself from responding to a speaker's words may not be entirely true of listeners who are insane, drugged, hypnotized, seriously retarded, too young to understand the consequences of their actions, or somehow under the physical control of the speaker. In those unusual situations, I see less of a problem likening provocative or inciting utterances to triggers and fires or even calling them speech acts. But the First Amendment was not designed with the insane, the enslaved, or the mentally incapacitated in mind, and I reject the idea that we should build our normal law of communication around them.

4

Hate Speech

Few would dispute the observation that one of the most visible and pressing problems of our time is the apparent upsurge of incidents of hate speech and hate crimes in our streets and neighborhoods, our workplaces, and even our high schools and colleges. Members of groups including native Americans, African Americans, Hispanic Americans, Asian Americans, and Arab Americans, Jews, gay men, and lesbians have been among the victims. State legislatures and city councils have enacted new laws against hate crimes;[1] police departments have set up special units to deal with them; Congress has mandated the compilation of statistics on the matter;[2] and schools have initiated everything from sensitivity training to speech codes to try to address the problem.

Although I will not engage in an analysis of the causes of this problem, many possibilities have been suggested by other writers. Economic insecurity is usually a factor, if not the most powerful one, in producing this kind of scapegoating, as are lack of education, feelings of political powerlessness, and the implicit approval of group prejudice by people of influence. Other causes are more specific to particular groups, such as the Persian Gulf War with regard to Arabs, trade tensions with respect to the Japanese, resentment over affirmative action with regard to African Americans, and lack of confidence about one's own sexuality with respect to gay men and lesbians.

But it is not the causes of the problem nor even the possible solutions to be found in the realms of education or enforcement of the criminal law that I want to address. There are experts better qualified than I am to deal with those questions. Rather, I want to focus on the speech aspects of the subject—the expression of group hatred solely through words and symbols, and the words or symbols that reveal the motivation for hate crimes. The former is a problem of pure speech. The latter is a problem of criminal behavior in which speech is the clue to its origins, and the communication of a message to the world may be one of its purposes. I examine the First Amendment implications of both kinds of expression of group hatred—the first in this chapter and the second in the chapter that follows. At the same time, I intend to demonstrate that neither of these phenomena can, properly speaking, be considered speech acts.

The first hurdle to overcome in any discussion of these issues is the mind-set of those who do not distinguish between, on the one hand, *words* of hatred that are uttered or *symbols* of hatred that are displayed and, on the other hand, *acts* of racial, ethnic, religious, or sexual discrimination or physical abuse. It is not the same to refer to people as "niggers" or to wear white robes at a Ku Klux Klan rally as it is to deny African Americans equality of opportunity for jobs, education, or housing.

The second confusion that needs to be dispelled is the perception that an advertisement published in a student newspaper denying that the Holocaust ever happened belongs in the same category as a torrent of telephone calls to a Jewish man at all hours of the day and night for two weeks calling him a "kike" and threatening his well-being—both of which were actual incidents.

I am not suggesting that the hurling of racial epithets, the display of symbols of group hatred, and the propagation of maliciously false ideas about groups of people are harmless just because they are pure speech. But it is important to understand that the kinds of harm that may flow from such speech are significantly different from those suffered as a result of *actions* that discriminate against people or physically abuse them because of their race, religion, ethnicity, or sexual orientation.

Being denied a decent education, job, or place to live; being beaten up; or even having one's phone continually rung are tangible harms that are easily identified, objectively verifiable, and materially debilitating or destructive. Being the target of denigrating words and symbols or of ideas that plant the seeds of group hatred may be psychologically frightening, may cause one to feel intimidated even in the absence of a direct and immediate threat of physical harm, may stimulate feelings of self-doubt and second-class citizenship, and may lead to one's psychological withdrawal or physical escape from the environment in which the hate speech has occurred. But note that each of these potential consequences has been described with the word *may*. None of them are automatic or inevitable. Like the responses to all pure speech, these consequences are mediated by what goes on in the victim's mind; and that will vary according to the past experiences, psychological and physical strength, status, needs, and goals of each particular target. For each one who is frightened or intimidated there may be another who is infuriated and spurred to countermeasures. For each one whose self-confidence is shaken there may be another who sees the tormenters as the lesser human beings they surely are. For each one whose voice is silenced there are others who will talk back. For each one who retreats, emotionally or physically, from the scene, there may be others who will stay, perhaps more determined than ever to fight for their rights.

The line of reasoning I have presented runs directly counter to that offered by Charles Lawrence and other advocates of restrictions on hate speech who reject the very distinction I am making. To fairly evaluate the relative merit of the two positions, it is important to review Lawrence's comments on the point.

> The experience of being called "nigger," "spic," "Jap," or "kike" is like receiving a slap in the face. The injury is instantaneous. There is neither opportunity for intermediary reflection on the idea conveyed nor an opportunity for responsive speech. . . . A defining attribute of speech is that it appeals first to the mind of the hearer who can evaluate its truth or persuasiveness. The use of racial epithets lacks this quality; it is a form of "violence by speech." . . . There is a great diffference between the offensiveness of words that you would rather not hear because they are labeled dirty, impolite, or personally demeaning—and the *injury* inflicted by words that remind the world that you are fair game for physical attack, evoke in you all the millions of cultural lessons regarding your inferiority that you have painstakingly repressed, and imprint upon you a badge of servitude and subservience for all the world to see.[3]

The flaws in the Lawrence position should be apparent. To say that being the target of racial or ethnic epithets is like receiving a slap in the face is to take the same poetic license as do those who liken so-called fighting words to knocking a chip off someone's shoulder. Physical acts are not like words except in a metaphorical sense.

Nor is the injury "instantaneous," as Lawrence asserts, with no "opportunity for intermediary reflection on the idea nor an opportunity for responsive speech." The fact that Lawrence, perhaps inadvertently although quite correctly, uses the word *idea* in this phrase gives away his argument. If it is the *idea* communicated by an epithet that hurts the victim, which it clearly is, that hurt will not be felt until the meaning of the utterance, along with all of its negative associations, has been processed through the brain. That can happen very rapidly, and *instantaneous* may even be an appropriate description if it is not taken to mean that it is *automatic* or, with the Lawrence gloss, that there is no opportunity for intermediary reflection. Any time the mind processes a communication, it is acting as an intermediary between stimulus and response, and that means reflection is taking place, even if it is only for a split second and is *almost* automatic.

I could not agree more with the Lawrence premise that "a defining attribute of speech is that it appeals first to the mind of the hearer who can evaluate its truth or persuasiveness." Nor could I disagree more, for the reasons just given, with his conclusion that "the use of epithets lacks this quality" and is a "form of 'violence by speech.'" The phrase *violence by speech* has a superficially plausible ring to it, but is in fact a contradiction in terms. As for his contention that epithets provide no "opportunity for responsive speech," I simply fail to see why that is so.

One cannot help but be sympathetic to the emotional thrust of the last sentence of the Lawrence quotation. It indisputably articulates the injury *often felt* by members of groups who have suffered a long history of discrimination and subjugation when they are confronted with abusive communication. Such speech may well evoke "all the millions of cultural lessons" of alleged racial inferiority that have been "painstakingly repressed" and that pin upon the victim a label of "servitude and subservience for all the world to see." Such speech may even, as Lawrence suggests, "remind the world" that the target is "fair game for physical attack," though that is a somewhat more distant possibility. But all of these injuries are psychological and emotional, perhaps felt more intensely, as Lawrence suggests, than would be the case in response to merely "dirty" or "impolite" words, but subjective nonetheless.

To conclude, as I have, that harms—or injuries, if one prefers—that are psychological and subjective in nature are different from objectively verifiable physical injuries does not answer the question as to whether those harms are great enough, and other considerations sufficiently compelling, to justify prohibiting what would otherwise be speech that is protected by the First Amendment. To address that question adequately involves asking not only whether emotional distress is too elusive to be a basis for the imposition of legal sanctions, but whether the banning of hate speech would be counterproductive and whether there are better remedies than the law for dealing with demeaning speech and delusional ideas. I turn to those issues now.

Although the intentional infliction of emotional distress by communicative behavior has long been recognized in the common law as a tort—a wrong—for which one can be sued, the traditional interpretation of that tort by English and American courts was that the victim could win such a suit only when the stimulus had been followed by palpable injury, such as a heart attack or a physiological nervous breakdown.[4] It is primarily in recent times that victims occasionally have been able to recover damages for mental or emotional distress in the absence of physical consequences. But those cases usually have occurred in special circumstances where, for example, the target of abuse is a customer or client on a railroad train, in a hotel, theatre, or amusement park and the abuser is an employee of that enterprise,[5] or where the communication has come from persons in positions of authority and has been directed to individuals under their power. A dramatic illustration of the latter occurred in a Minnesota high school when a female student who was summoned to the principal's office was falsely accused of unchastity and told that she could be imprisoned for her alleged immoral behavior. Although the facts of the case did not sustain her law suit for assault and slander, she did win damages for her charge of intentional infliction of emotional distress.[6]

In the discussion of so-called situation-altering utterances in chapter 2, I have shown how authority introduces potential consequences into a relationship that are not present in symbolic transactions between peers and thus gives to the utterances of persons in positions of authority a weight greater than the words themselves. When a boss or teacher indulges in racist remarks, the members of target groups under his or her supervision may reasonably conclude that they will not be treated fairly when task assignments are made or when raises, promotions, or grades are passed out. Institutional restrictions on such speech by employees who wield power over others is thus a justified, and even necessary, kind of social control over potential abuses of authority.

However, when it comes to interpersonal communication between peers or to messages promulgated to the public at large, the use of legal sanctions for the intentional infliction of emotional distress is much more problematic. The only case directly relevant to these matters decided thus far by the Supreme Court involved a target who was a prominent public figure, Jerry Falwell; and in that circumstance the Court had little trouble deciding unanimously that a legal remedy would violate the First Amendment. Falwell had been the butt of a tongue-in-cheek cartoon (that was clearly labeled as such) in the November 1983 issue of *Hustler* magazine, portraying his having a drunken, incestuous rendezvous with his mother in an outhouse. This was the Court's response to Falwell's complaint:

> Generally speaking the law does not regard the intent to inflict emotional distress as one which should receive much solicitude, and it is quite understandable that most if not all jurisdictions have chosen to make it civilly culpable where the conduct in question is sufficiently "outrageous." . . . [Falwell] contends . . . that the caricature in question here was so "outrageous" as to distinguish it from more traditional political cartoons. There is no doubt that the caricature of respondent and his mother published in Hustler is at best a distant cousin of the political cartoons described above, and a rather poor relation at that. If it were possible by laying down a principled standard to separate the one from the other, public discourse would probably suffer little or no harm. But we doubt that there is any such standard, and we are quite sure that the pejorative description "outrageous" does not supply one. "Outrageousness" in the area of political and social discourse has an inherent subjectiveness about it which would allow a jury to impose liability on the basis of the jurors' tastes or views, or perhaps on the basis of their dislike of a particular expression. An "outrageousness" standard thus runs afoul of our longstanding refusal to allow damages to be awarded because the speech in question may have an adverse emotional impact on the audience.[7]

Although the Court, in the Falwell case, made it impossible for public figures to successfully sue for the intentional infliction of emotional distress without first proving that the communication in question was also a knowing or reckless falsehood, and thus subject to damages for defamation, the justices avoided the broader question as to whether the same principle would apply to private persons. Yet the logic of their decision would seem to compel that result. The subjectivity of emotional reactions is not unique to public figures, nor to political and social discourse, and what outrages one private person who is the target of abusive speech may not outrage another. Whether or not the Supreme Court actually proceeds to this logical conclusion at some time in the future, I believe that a proper interpretation of the First Amendment would require it to do so.

The elusiveness of the concept of emotional distress and its potential for misuse, whether by a public or a private person, was illustrated at the time of the attempted neo-Nazi march in Skokie, Illinois in 1977–78. Among the several law suits filed in an attempt to prevent that march, one alleged that if the demonstration were allowed to take place it would inflict emotional suffering on Holocaust survivors who were exposed to it. The lead plaintiff in that suit testified in court that the sight of men marching in Nazi uniforms with Nazi symbols would evoke intolerably painful memories of the execution of his parents and should therefore be prohibited. Yet further testimony revealed that he had gone willingly to observe other neo-Nazi rallies in the Chicago area and to engage in counterdemonstrations against them. The emotional distress he claimed he would experience as the result of a march in Skokie was evidently more anger than hurt and, in any event, certainly had not silenced or immobilized him.

Even if one were to concede (which I do not) that the emotional distress some victims of hate speech experience is sufficiently serious, predictable, and verifiable to make legal remedies a feasible and justified response, questions remain whether such remedies are counterproductive and whether they are the most effective way of dealing with the problem.

Several practical consequences to the banning of hate speech should give pause to anyone attracted to that solution. First and foremost, suppressing the overt verbal or symbolic expression of group hatred does not make the attitudes that give rise to such expression go away. Most probably, the people who hold such attitudes will move underground, where their hatred will fester and possibly erupt in a more violent form at a later time. Since an unseen enemy is more dangerous and more difficult to defend against than one that is visible, it seems foolish to drive such bigots into hiding.

Not all racists will go underground if their most vitriolic speech is curbed. Those who are verbally skilled enough will express their hatred in more indirect and sophisticated ways, thus evading the letter of the law and at the same time increasing the persuasiveness of their message by phrasing it in less repugnant terms. This is exactly what occurred in Great Britain with a racist journal after passage of the British Racial Relations Act of 1965. That law made it illegal to publish any "threatening, abusive, or insulting" material that aimed at fomenting "hatred against any section of the public in Great Britain distinguished by color, race, ethnic or national origins."[8] When the law went into effect the racist journal kept the same message but cleaned up its language. The result was an increase in its circulation!

It is not necessary to cross the Atlantic Ocean to witness this same phenomenon. One only need look to Louisiana where a scrubbed-up version of David Duke came frighteningly close to being elected governor of that state and thereupon launched a campaign for the presidency of the United States. Indeed, a lesson we should have learned from recent, supposedly more respectable, presidential and senatorial candidates is that coded messages of group hatred that steer wide of what could be outlawed by any conceivable ban on hate speech are potentially far more harmful to disadvantaged groups than anything a ranting and raving racist might say. Yet no one would suggest that, so long as we have a First Amendment, anything in the way of legal limitations can be done about such speech.

Prohibitions also turn censored material into "forbidden fruit" and the advocates of racism into martyrs. Whenever any communication—a book, essay, speech, rally, film, play, or work of art—is banned, some persons will suppose it contains a potent and important message that the censors fear, else why would they seek to suppress it? Thus, it arouses more interest than if it had been ignored. Curiosity, if nothing else, will lead some to try to find out for themselves what is being withheld from them.

The would-be communicators whose speech is prohibited also gain more publicity and, quite possibly, more sympathy than they could otherwise hope to achieve. The attempt to prohibit the neo-Nazi march in Skokie brought more attention to Frank Collin, their leader, and to his message, than he could ever have dreamed of achieving on his own. The electoral successes in France of National Front leader Jean-Marie Le Pen may well be due, in part, to the role of martyr he has played to the hilt as a result of the various legal actions brought against him under French law for "inciting racial hatred."

Legal limitations on hate speech are not only likely to be counterproductive, they are simply not the most effective way to deal with the problem. If there is any hope of changing the attitudes of the haters, it can only come, in the short run, from exposing them to more enlightened ways of thinking and, in the long run, through alleviating the causes of their insecurity. Supreme Court Justice Louis Brandeis, in a famous opinion written in 1927, captured the essence of the First Amendment's answer to hate speech when he said: "If there be time to expose through discussion the falsehood and fallacies, to avert the evil by the processes of education, the remedy to be applied is more speech, not enforced silence. Only an emergency can justify repression. Such must be the rule if authority is to be reconciled with freedom. Such, in my opinion, is the command of the Constitution."[9]

5

Hate Crimes

I turn now to examine the second problem indicated at the outset of the previous chapter, hate crimes. These are criminal acts motivated by group hatred, ranging all the way from trespass and defacement of property to assault and battery, arson, and murder. There are two reasons for considering the possibility that the First Amendment may be implicated in criminal convictions for such offenses. The first is that one purpose of the criminal act, if not the primary purpose, may be to send a political or social message to the world, such as a warning that African Americans are not welcome in a particular neighborhood, or that gay men had better go back into the closet or else risk physical harm. The second reason is that the only way to identify group hatred as the motivation is by statements the perpetrator has made or by other symbolic behavior engaged in before, during, or after the commission of the crime.

Neither of these reasons justifies calling the crimes speech acts, any more than a bank robbery becomes a speech act because one of the gunmen speaks to the tellers and orders them to "stick 'em up." These are physical behaviors with speech ingredients, just the converse of an oration, which is speech behavior with the physical ingredient of noise. But whereas the noise made by a speech does not usually cause us to believe that the speech should be suppressed, the speech involved in a hate crime *may* cause us to think that penalties greater than what would normally apply to such a crime are justified. That is the First Amendment puzzle I intend to address and that the Supreme Court was addressing as this book went to press.[1] The Court was apparently impelled to swifter than usual action on this matter because so many cities and states have adopted "ethnic intimidation" or hate crime laws that impose stiffer penalties on crimes committed out of group hatred than are imposed on the same crimes when that motivation is not present. The rationale ordinarily offered for this differential treatment is that hate crimes pose a more serious danger to society than equivalent crimes that are not bias-motivated. Hate crimes harm not only the particular victims of the act, but society in general, by aggravating intergroup tensions, spreading fear throughout the communities of which the victims are members, and possibly encouraging copycat crimes to a greater extent than does run-of-the-mill criminal behavior.

In those instances where these laws have been challenged in state or lower federal courts, some have been upheld, but some have been struck down on First Amendment grounds. Thus, we must ask if there are countervailing free speech interests that should cause us to refrain from combating these dangers by imposing enhanced penalties on crimes motivated by group hatred. The first question I raised above is whether the act should be entitled to First Amendment protection if it has been committed for the sole or primary purpose of sending a message to the world, with the immediate target being perhaps an incidental or random victim. This claim cannot be taken seriously. Trespass, defacement or destruction of property, assault and battery, arson, and murder are made criminal by the law because of the substantial physical harm they do to their victims. Those harms occur regardless of any possible communicative purposes the perpetrator may have had in mind, and those purposes cannot be accepted as an excuse for the behavior if a safe and peaceful society is to be maintained.

Where the offense in question is arguably a victimless crime with no palpable injury to others, and the purpose is to communicate a message, one cannot be so cavalier in dismissing a free speech claim. But that is true whether the alleged offender seeks First Amendment protection against an *enhanced* penalty for a bias-motivated act or against *any* penalty for any behavior that would normally be punishable. Since the punishment of victimless crimes committed for the purpose of communication raises broader issues than enhanced penalties for hate crimes, a full discussion of those questions is reserved for chapter 8.

The second free speech concern about enhanced penalties for hate crimes is indeed a serious one, for the only way one can know that a hate crime has been committed is if the perpetrators have revealed their motivation by expressing it verbally or symbolically. If a gang of hoodlums jumps out of a car and beats up a gay man on the sidewalk, at the same time yelling, "You lousy queer," or if swastikas are painted on a temple wall, we know that a hate crime has been committed. But if those same hoodlums beat up a gay man and say nothing and give no evidence in their previous statements that they were looking for gay men to beat up, or if graffiti with no clear meaning is scrawled on a temple wall, we have no way of knowing or proving a group hatred motivation. Thus, it might fairly be claimed, and has been claimed, that to impose heavier penalties on those who have expressed racist views than on those who have kept their views to themselves is to punish the former for their beliefs and their speech, in violation of the First Amendment.

A state court judge in Michigan made this argument in strong language when he found that state's ethnic intimidation law to be unconstitutional. The case involved a defendant charged with both arson and ethnic intimidation in the burning of the home of an African American family. While letting the arson charge stand, the judge dismissed the ethnic intimidation charge on the grounds that the state statute was both vague and violative of the First Amendment:

> It is claimed that the statute punishes conduct rather than words or expression. This argument has a hollow ring, as the punishable conduct, namely physical contact or damaging, destroying, or defacing real or personal property, is already punishable under other criminal statutes. What is punished is the spoken or written word or expression thereof by conduct. There are numerous instances where this statute can be applied to convert conduct, which would normally be a misdemeanor, into a felony merely because of the spoken word. For example, A strikes B in the face with his fists thereby committing a misdemeanor commonly known as assault and battery. However, should A add just one word, such as "kraut," "wop," "frog," "honkie," "nigger," "bitch," "Hebrew," "queer," it becomes a felony; and A will be punished not for his conduct alone, a misdemeanor, but for using the spoken word.[2]

It is of additional interest that in this case the evidence that the crime was motivated by group hatred came not from any statements directed at the victims or from any utterances made to others before or during the commission of the act, but from remarks the defendant made to friends after the fact, when he was apparently drunk.[3]

There is no getting around the argument that enhanced penalties for hate crimes do, indeed, punish people, in part, for the verbal or symbolic expression of their beliefs and attitudes. But whether that should automatically be considered a violation of their First Amendment rights, as the Michigan judge and others have concluded, is a very different matter. To begin with, they are, or should be, punished only when their beliefs and attitudes have resulted in the commission of a crime. Moreover, those beliefs and attitudes are the basis only for judging the severity of their crime and the appropriate degree of punishment, not for deciding whether they will be punished at all. Enhanced penalties for hate crimes are arguably comparable to the differences in punishment among first-degree murder, second-degree murder, and manslaughter, where the victim is just as dead, but the motivation or state of mind of the killer determines the gravity of the crime and the punishment. If the killing occurred in self-defense, which is another state of mind, it does not even constitute a crime, for the *mens rea* (bad mind) required by the law is missing. Although there are serious hazards to the fair administration of justice any time a court probes into the state of mind of those charged with criminal acts, and particularly when dealing with attitudes like group hatred, it is a necessary enterprise if one accepts the premise, as I do, that bias-motivated crimes pose a greater danger to the peace and safety of society than equivalent crimes that are not so motivated.

Yet before concluding that the harms done to society by hate crimes are sufficient to justify the possible invasions of sacred First Amendment territory that enhanced penalties might entail, one should assess what those potential intrusions are and the extent to which they can be avoided by carefully drafted and carefully administered enhanced penalty laws. Two possible dangers to First Amendment rights that arise when group hatred is used as a basis for enhanced penalties are well illustrated in a pair of cases decided by the Supreme Court in 1992.

The first was a case in which a white convict, David Dawson, while escaping from a Delaware state prison, murdered a white woman and stole her car. Dawson was sentenced to death for this crime after the prosecution told the jury that he belonged to a white racist prison gang called the Aryan Brotherhood. That sentence, which was upheld by the Delaware Supreme Court, was appealed to the U.S. Supreme Court on the grounds that Dawson's membership in the Aryan Brotherhood was a First Amendment activity that was irrelevant to the crime he had committed and was therefore a constitutionally impermissible consideration in determining his punishment. Eight justices of the U.S. Supreme Court agreed and sent the case back to the Supreme Court of Delaware for either a new sentencing procedure that excluded the evidence of his Aryan Brotherhood membership or a finding that the use of this evidence constituted a "harmless error" that had not been determinative in the making of the death penalty decision.[4]

Chief Justice William Rehnquist's opinion for the Court stressed that the use of "associational evidence," such as Dawson's membership in a racist group, to help determine a sentence would be acceptable if it were either relevant to the crime itself or were an indication of the defendant's propensity to violence. But, he said, "On the present record one is left with the feeling that the Aryan Brotherhood evidence was employed simply because the jury would find these beliefs morally reprehensible," and that such a use was a "constitutional error."[5]

The State of Delaware had argued, on the other hand, that Dawson's membership in the Aryan Brotherhood constituted an aggravating circumstance worthy of consideration by the jury and that its introduction was warranted to offset the defense's claims as to his good character. Justice Clarence Thomas, the lone Supreme Court dissenter, agreed that Dawson's membership "had relevance at sentencing" because the jury could reasonably conclude from it "that he had engaged in some sort of forbidden activities while in prison."[6] Justice Thomas also agreed that the prosecutors were entitled to as much leeway in attempting to establish the defendant's bad character as the defense had in presenting a picture of Dawson as a person of good character who had earned credit for good behavior while in prison.

Not only does the very loose position taken by the State of Delaware and by Justice Thomas illustrate the potential hazard to the exercise of First Amendment rights in the use of speech or associational evidence of group hatred as a basis for determining the severity of criminal punishments. Even the Supreme Court's majority opinion, while far more sensitive to, and protective of, the First Amendment interests at stake, opens the door wider than is desirable to the use of a defendant's ideological beliefs and associations. For it admits them as indicators of a vague propensity to violent criminal behavior.

The second recent Supreme Court case that illuminates the First Amendment pitfalls in laws against hate crimes and in their enforcement is *R.A.V. v. St. Paul*, in which a juvenile burned a cross on the lawn of an African American family. He was charged with both fourth-degree assault—a charge that was not contested when he took his case to the Supreme Court—and with bias-motivated disorderly conduct, in violation of a city ordinance that the trial court judge found to be unconstitutional. The St. Paul ordinance at issue provided that "whoever places on public or private property a symbol, object, appellation, characterization or graffiti, including but not limited to, a burning cross or Nazi swastika, which one knows or has reasonable grounds to know arouses anger, alarm, or resentment in others on the basis of race, color, creed, religion, or gender commits disorderly conduct and shall be guilty of a misdemeanor."[7]

In reversing the trial court and upholding the ordinance, the Minnesota Supreme Court did not dispute the claim that, as written, the law intruded into areas of expression that are protected by the First Amendment. It acknowledged that the "ordinance should have been more carefully drafted,"[8] but chose to save it by a limiting interpretation that would allow its enforcement only against expression that either constitutes fighting words or is intended and likely to produce imminent lawless action.

But this decision did not satisfy those who succeeded in persuading the U.S. Supreme Court to accept the case for review. They argued that the ordinance was too fatally flawed to be saved—still vague and overbroad even as doctored by the Minnesota Supreme Court. As the *amicus curiae* brief of the American Civil Liberties Union and American Jewish Congress put it, "The purported limiting construction adopted by the Minnesota Supreme Court is necessarily colored by its view that '[t]he burning cross is itself an unmistakable symbol of violence and hatred based on virulent notions of racial supremacy.'"[9]

A unanimous Supreme Court agreed that the St. Paul ordinance was unconstitutional.[10] A five-person majority of the justices, although feeling bound by the Minnesota Supreme Court's narrowing construction that the ordinance proscribed only fighting words, found it still in violation of the First Amendment. For although allegedly limited to fighting words, the law appeared to be applicable only to those fighting words that insult or provoke violence "on the basis of race, color, creed, religion, or gender." That, in the majority's view, was a form of content and viewpoint discrimination disallowed by the First Amendment, even if within a category of speech (fighting words) that could be totally prohibited.[11]

The remaining four Supreme Court justices were appalled at the majority's view that the government could not single out a subcategory of otherwise unprotected speech for special penalties. But since they agreed with the argument made by the petitioner that, despite the Minnesota Supreme Court's effort to save it, the ordinance was still "fatally overbroad because it criminalizes not only unprotected expression but . . . expressive conduct that causes only hurt feelings, offense, or resentment,"[12] they concurred in the Court's final judgment.

Because the St. Paul ordinance struck down by the Supreme Court was not strictly speaking a law that enhanced penalties for hate *crimes*, but a law restricting pure speech and symbolic behavior, it may not seem directly relevant to the present discussion. However, it functioned like a hate crime law in this instance by virtue of its being invoked as a second count, which allowed additional penalty for a group hatred motivation, on top of a first count of ordinary assault. It was indeed that aspect of the case that induced the concurring Supreme Court justices to part company from a majority opinion that might be interpreted to imply that society could not deal more severely with hate crimes than with offenses otherwise motivated. But the phrasing of some of their reservations demonstrates how easily the hate crime concept, if not carefully circumscribed, can spill over into free speech terrain. Justice White, for example, opined that "the majority legitimates hate speech as a form of public discussion."[13] Justice Blackmun saw "great harm in preventing the people of St. Paul from specifically punishing the race-based fighting words that so prejudice their community."[14] And Justice Stevens would find it "legitimate" and "reasonable" to have "special rules" which punish "threatening someone because of her race or religious beliefs . . . more severely than threats against someone based on, say, his support of a particular athletic team."[15]

Additional dangers to freedom of speech posed by the imposition of enhanced penalties for bias-motivated crimes have been well articulated by Susan Gellman in a 1991 law review article on the subject.[16] Using as her point of departure the model hate crimes statute recommended by the Anti-Defamation League of B'nai B'rith, the language of which has been tracked by many jurisdictions, Gellman begins her critique by noting some serious problems of vagueness in such legislation. She concedes, however, that some of these flaws can probably be cured by more precise drafting.[17]

Her first point about vagueness is that the model statute turns on "the actual or perceived race, color, national origin or sexual orientation of *another individual or individuals*." Her objection to this is as follows:

> Presumably, this would include cases in which the direct victim(s) of the underlying offense are of a different ethnicity than the offender. It is probably also intended to include cases in which the offender and the direct victim are of the same ethnicity, turning upon the ethnicity of a third party having some relationship to the victim, the offender, or both, or to the incident: for example, where *A*, a white man, angered by the sight of *B*, another white man, kissing an African-American woman, *C*, threatens *B*. It is far less likely that the statute is intended to reach the case in which *A*, a white woman, hearing *B*, another white woman, calling *C*, an African-American man, a racist name, threatens *B* in an attempt to protect *C*. Yet in both the case of the "racist meddler" and the case of the "anti-racist champion," *C*'s race is equally at issue. Finally, it is completely unclear whether the statute would reach a case in which the ethnicity of completely unrelated persons was at issue: one Jew threatening another in an argument about Louis Farrakhan, one white harassing another for his support of Nelson Mandela, one African-American destroying another's poster of Madonna, one gay breaking another's Anita Bryant records.[18]

Gellman's second vagueness concern has to do with "mixed motive situations":

> The statute requires that the offender acted "by reason of" the ethnicity of another, but it does not state whether that person's ethnicity must be the *sole* reason for the offender's actions, whether it must be the *predominant* reason, or whether it may

be merely a *substantial* reason, a *significant* reason, a *contributing* reason, a *barely existing* reason, or an *objectively possible* reason. The "by reason of" language being the only element added to those of the underlying offenses, the statute's failure to specify just how much of a reason for the commission of the offense the ethnicity of another must be provides inadequate notice of what is proscribed.[19]

Finally, she identifies a vagueness problem she doubts can be solved by more careful drafting:

If a statute following the ADL model is read as doing nothing more than enhancing the penalty for an existing non-vague crime because of the actor's bias motive, it may survive a vagueness challenge, but it then criminalizes pure thought. If, on the other hand, it is argued that the presence of the bias motive changes the qualitative character of the underlying crime so drastically that it becomes an entirely different act, then the statute may be held void for vagueness, because it can no longer rely upon the understood meaning of the predicate offense for notice of proscribed behavior. In other words, if the statute does not criminalize pure motive, because the sum of the act plus the motive is greater than its parts, that "sum" is not defined by the statute, and the statute is unconstitutionally vague.[20]

In addition to her vagueness concerns, Gellman also argues that "the model statute invites discriminatory enforcement, including application to members of a racial minority who may aggressively refer to police officers as 'honky cops.' Furthermore, any time one of the underlying offenses is committed, and the offender and the victim happen to be of different ethnicities, there will be the risk of even well-meaning officers and prosecutors adding a charge of ethnic intimidation as well."[21]

Let me now review the possible incursions that may be made into protected First Amendment territory by enhanced penalties for bias-motivated offenses and attempt to determine if they are sufficiently serious or inevitable to warrant rejecting this particular approach to the hate crime problem.

The danger posed by the irrelevant introduction into a trial or sentencing procedure of a criminal defendant's ideology and associations such as occurred in the lower courts in *Dawson v. Delaware* has now been largely foreclosed by the Supreme Court's decision in that case. Although the Court left open the possibility of unacceptable intrusions on freedom of speech and association in the use of a defendant's past First Amendment activity as an indicator of his or her commitment to violence or potential dangerousness, such intrusions could easily be prevented.

To begin with, they could be foreclosed by the law making absolutely clear that a defendant's group associations or expressions of belief not directly and immediately related to the crime are inadmissible as evidence that a hate crime has been committed. For example, the law could specify, as does California's hate crime statute, that no one can be convicted of a bias crime "upon speech alone, except upon a showing that the speech itself threatened violence against a specific person or group of persons and that the defendant had the apparent ability to carry out the threat."[22] Finally, the law could require the prosecution to prove beyond a reasonable doubt that the defendant intentionally selected the victim on the basis of that victim's actual or perceived race, ethnicity, religion, or sexual orientation.

As for the problem presented by the St. Paul ordinance, I need only repeat that the introduction into a hate crime situation of an unconstitutionally overbroad restriction on purely symbolic behavior to bump up the penalty for that crime did more than violate the First Amendment. It also muddied the waters with regard to what might constitute bona fide enhanced penalties for a physical offense that is bias-motivated. We need not be distracted from that issue by the St. Paul red herring.

With respect to the concerns expressed by Gellman, I noted her concession that some of the vagueness problems infecting enhanced penalty statutes can probably be cured by more precise drafting. Enhanced penalties can be limited, for example, to crimes where the perpetrator is of a different race, religion, ethnicity, or sexual orientation than the victim. The ambiguities suggested by Gellman in same-ethnicity situations would thus be eliminated, but the most egregious instances of hate crimes would still be reached.

For what she describes as "mixed motive situations," enhanced penalty laws could simply specify that stiffer penalties would be triggered only in those cases where group hatred was the sole or predominant reason for the offender's action, thus excluding those situations where the particular victim was targeted for individualized reasons in addition to his or her race, religion, ethnicity, or sexual orientation. Alternatively, a statute's authors could choose to cast a wider net and specify that if a victim's group identity was a contributing reason for the crime, then enhanced penalties would apply. Such breadth is probably not necessary to deal with the most serious hate crimes and should be avoided for that reason, but it could finesse the vagueness criticisr...

The alleged vagueness problem that Gellman believes cannot be fixed by precision drafting is, in my judgment, a straw man. She asserts that we have an either-or choice, an assertion that I believe to be fallacious. We can have either a nonvague statute that "criminalizes pure thought," she says, or a law that punishes some inevitably vague "sum" of an act that is partly speech and partly conduct. But I would suggest that those are not the alternatives. Rather, a well-crafted enhanced penalty law would specify that the only offenses to be punished are those *acts* that would normally qualify as criminal behavior—assault and battery, arson, murder, and so on—and that enhanced penalties would be triggered only when those *acts* have been demonstrably motivated by group hatred.

Gellman would no doubt respond that in such circumstances the enhanced penalties do criminalize pure thought, just as the trial judge in the Michigan case referred to earlier claimed that under his state's ethnic intimidation statute a misdemeanor could be converted into a felony "merely because of the spoken word." But it would not be merely because of the spoken word or because of pure thought that the bumped up penalty has been triggered. It would be because, and only because, those thoughts, and the words that have revealed them, have led to criminal actions. Nor do those actions now constitute some vague new crime or sum that is greater than its parts, as Gellman suggests. They are the very same acts as might have been committed for reasons other than group hatred, but the aggravating circumstance of a group hatred motivation has been deemed by the law to require more severe punishment. I can further clarify my point by responding to an example that Gellman uses to advance her position. She argues that the federal civil rights laws dealing with discrimination in employment, housing, and education provide no precedent for penalizing bias-motivated crimes because "discrimination and bigotry are not the same thing; the former is an illegal act, the latter is a constitutionally protected (albeit odious) attitude. Just as bigotry can exist without being acted upon, discrimination can occur without racist motivation. It is the discriminatory action, and not the racial motive, that Congress intended to prohibit in those statutes."[23]

I submit that Gellman is flat wrong in the concluding two sentences of this quotation. Although her premise is entirely valid—that bigotry can exist without action being taken on it, and that discrimination can occur without racist motivation—I would point out that nothing is wrong with discrimination that is not based on group prejudice. To discriminate among students, based on their academic performance, when giving out grades or awarding honors, or to discriminate among employees for raises or promotion on the basis of their work record, or to choose to spend social time with some people and not others because one has more fun with the former than the latter, is perfectly reasonable and justified. It is only what is called *invidious* discrimination, based on irrelevant, stereotyped, or prejudiced criteria, that is unjustified and, in the case of racial, ethnic, or sexual stereotypes used in the making of employment or housing choices, illegal. Thus, when Gellman says of the federal civil rights laws that it is "the discriminatory action, and not the racial animus, that is prohibited," she is mistaken. It is only discrimination based on group animus that is prohibited. That is no more, and no less, a prohibition based on the beliefs and attitudes of the perpetrator of invidious discrimination than enhanced penalties for the commission of hate crimes.

Like Gellman, I too have concerns about the discriminatory enforcement that may occur when hate crime laws are on the books, but my concerns are somewhat different from hers. I do not see a unique problem, for instance, with the police invoking such laws more readily against the members of disadvantaged, than advantaged, groups. Such discrimination is a serious but generic problem of *all* law enforcement and needs to be addressed at that broader level, not solely with respect to the enforcement of hate crime laws. I am also not as troubled as she is by the possibility that "well-meaning officers and prosecutors" may add a charge of ethnic intimidation any time a crime is committed by a person of one ethnicity against a victim of another group. If the law enforcement officials are really well-meaning, that is not likely to happen unless they have some reason to believe that group hatred was the stimulus for the crime.

What does concern me a great deal is a kind of discriminatory enforcement that Gellman does not mention. It is the fact that only those offenders who are outspoken about their group biases and hatreds will be subjected to enhanced penalties for their crimes, whereas those who may have had exactly the same motivation, but kept their beliefs and attitudes to themselves, will escape the added punishment. This concern is somewhat alleviated by my assumption that most group haters who commit criminal acts are not likely to be secretive about their attitudes and motivations. For one thing, it would be very difficult for them never to have revealed those attitudes and motivations to other people who might become potential witnesses against them. On the contrary, they are more likely to be proud of their views and actions and to want them to be known, at least in circles they presume to be sympathetic.

But perhaps more important is the fact that if the purpose of their crime is to send a political or social message to the world, that message may not get across unless they accompany their action with words or symbols that reveal its motivation. If they beat up a gay man and say nothing, paint meaningless graffiti on a temple wall, or set fire to the home of an African American family without simultaneously communicating some kind of verbal warning to other African Americans, their criminal act may speak for itself, but that would require a particular inference being made by the public, an inference that may not have been clearly indicated. If offenders want to be sure to get their message across, they are more likely to make it verbally or symbolically explicit.

Having said all this, I still recognize the problem that those who speak out most clearly about their hatreds will be the ones subjected to enhanced penalties, and those who are smart enough, or devious enough, to successfully hide their motivations will not be. It reminds me of the situation a number of years ago after Congress enacted the requirement that all young men register for the draft on reaching their eighteenth birthday. Apparently, several thousand men, out of conscience or negligence, did not comply with this requirement, but only a relatively small number of them—primarily those who had spoken out publicly against the law—were prosecuted by the government. The argument was made in their defense that this selective pattern of law enforcement was a violation of the First Amendment because punishment was being meted out only to those who had exercised their freedom of speech. Whether it should have or not, that argument failed to win judicial agreement. The men who were prosecuted were, after all, in clear violation of the law, and the fact that other violators were not also pursued was viewed as entirely within the discretion of prosecuting officials, just as prosecutions for all offenses are ultimately left to the discretion of law enforcement officers.

I return now to the large question posed at the outset of this chapter. Are there countervailing free speech interests that should cause us to refrain from combating the dangers that hate crimes pose to society by imposing enhanced penalties on such behavior? Those dangers should not be minimized. In addition to the injury they inflict on their immediate targets, hate crimes exacerbate already hazardous racial and ethnic tensions, and may engender fear in members of victim groups to the point that they hesitate to walk on the sidewalks of their own community or venture into the territory of others to work, to live, or to engage in their other normal pursuits. In weighing those harms against the relatively minimal intrusions into the First Amendment arena that a carefully drafted enhanced penalty law may entail, I come hesitantly to the conclusion that such laws are constitutionally acceptable. As to whether they are wise as a matter of public policy, I am quite unsure and thus leave that question for others to answer.[24]

6

Sexist Speech

A discussion of sexist speech and sexist acts—generally directed from men toward women but once in a while occurring in reverse—might well have been incorporated into the two previous chapters, since these behaviors are, in many respects, expressions of a kind of group hatred. But they are also different in significant ways from bigoted behavior toward people of minority races, religions, ethnicity, and sexual orientation. For one, they usually spring less from hatred than from such sources as insensitivity, stereotyped thinking, or psychological needs to put or keep oneself in a dominant position.

Furthermore, women are not a minority in society at large. In most places, and in most age groups, they actually constitute a slight numerical majority. One significant result of this in a democracy like the United States is that, if they use it, they have more voting power than men. Yet it is also true that in many of the most influential arenas of life they are a distinct minority, such as the higher levels of business and government and the faculties of leading universities. As a result they experience the same disadvantages in those contexts as do the members of real minority groups.

Finally, women have, and have always had, certain areas of power and channels of influence that have not been available to other victims of discrimination. Frequently, important decisions regarding home and family that can have far-reaching impact are left entirely in their hands or at least are shared with them. Men in positions of power in society are also often significantly influenced in their thinking and actions by the women in their lives. Even if not significantly influenced, men have at least been exposed to the views of women, which is frequently not the case with other disadvantaged groups. None of this means that women suffer less from sexist speech and sexist acts when those behaviors occur than do other groups when they are subjected

49

to hate speech and hate crimes. It does mean that more resources are available to them to combat such behavior and that the prognosis for a better future is therefore somewhat brighter.

As in the previous exploration of hate speech and hate crimes, I begin discussing the problem of sexism by underscoring the distinction between speech and acts. Sexist speech may consist of everything from coarse, insensitive jokes and uninvited, unwanted sexual propositions to photographs and films that portray women in denigrating ways. Sexist acts, on the other hand, range all the way from uninvited and unwelcome touching, to unequal pay for equivalent work, to unfair sharing of homemaking chores, to glass ceilings in business and the professions, to rape, spouse beating, and other kinds of physical violence. Sexist acts are beyond the scope of this book. My focus is on sexist speech.

For purposes of clarity, I begin the analysis by dealing separately with speech that is personally addressed to an individual or small group of individuals in face-to-face encounters and with that addressed to the public or world at large through such media as books, magazines, posters, billboards, songs, movies, videotapes, live stage performances, radio, and television. Having done that I will be in a better position to examine those circumstances in which interpersonal and public communication may be combined to produce a generally sexist environment.

With respect to personal interactions, it is easy to identify certain kinds of speech that are not only clearly inappropriate but also qualify as sexual harassment that should be prohibited either by law or by rules of the institution in which they occur. First and foremost in this category would be statements to subordinates by persons in positions of authority offering rewards or threatening punishments with respect to promotions, salaries, grades, or task assignments if those subordinates do or do not agree to engage in sexual activities. Also in this category would be a persistent pattern of sexually provocative or sexually obsessive conversations by a superior with a subordinate, such as those Anita Hill alleged were made to her by her boss at the time, Clarence Thomas. A similarly persistent pattern of talk or gestures coming from a peer or group of peers in a work situation, where the target cannot extricate himself or herself from the scene, ought, after fair warning, to be equally prohibitable.

The issue becomes less clear in peer relationships where one person makes only an occasional comment indicating a sexual interest in the other person, remarking on some aspect of that individual's physique, telling a joke with sexual overtones, or even making an explicit sexual proposition. The complexity of the problem is well illustrated in a *New York Times* article about teenagers trying to cope with this matter:

> Following the lead of women in the workplace and on college campuses, female students in high schools and junior high schools are tentatively challenging the "boys will be boys" status quo. . . .
>
> "Girls are getting more and more aware of it," said Whitney Casey, a student at Monte Vista High School in Danville, Calif. "We're sick of men's comments. It needs to stop."
>
> The boys, for their part, are getting more and more confused. "Am I allowed to tell Whitney she has beautiful eyes?" asked Adam Saperstein, a classmate. "Where does it start and where does it stop?"
>
> Two recent court rulings, including one by the Supreme Court, have held schools liable for damages in sexual harassment cases, and at least one state—Minnesota—does the same. The Minnesota law defines sexual harassment as unwelcome sexual advances.
> . . .
>
> Litigating and legislating relations between teen-age boys and girls is hailed by some and condemned by others.
>
> Those who favor sanctions say that ignoring certain behavior sends a message of inequality to girls and of privilege to boys and sets the stage for how men and women treat each other as adults.
>
> "Girls are learning that they are second-class citizens, only valued for their physical attributes," said Sharon Schuster, president of the American Association of University Women, which recently issued a report that painted a damning picture of how girls are treated in school. "This has a terribly detrimental effect on girls—and on boys. They will never learn equal relationships unless they are told this is not appropriate."
>
> But others argue that applying adult rules to what many people consider teen-age high jinks is an overreaction.
>
> Bob Giannini, the principal at Monte Vista High, said that what may look like harassment is often just harmless adolescent exploration.
>
> And one of the male students at Monte Vista, Damon Bowers, described "this whole sexual harassment thing" as "propaganda."
> . . .
>
> Recent visits to a high school and junior high school in California made it clear that coarse remarks and gestures were widespread,

complicating what for most adolescents is an already confusing journey to sexual maturity. In conversations with more than 150 girls and boys at Monte Vista High in the Bay area and Stephens Middle School in Long Beach, virtually every student had experienced, witnessed or participated in such behavior.

Most of the girls said they were troubled by the boys' behavior but felt helpless to respond. "It might be so bad you want to ignore it," said one eighth grader. "It might be you don't know what to do so you act like it never happened." . . .

The boys, with a few defiant exceptions, were ignorant of the girls' feelings rather than malicious. They misunderstand, for instance, the difference btween a compliment and a crude remark. "There's a fine line; that's obvious to me now," one high school student said after a girl explained that she liked being told that her sweater was pretty but not that she had nice breasts.[1]

But it is not only adolescents who are on "a confusing journey to sexual maturity." The same can be said of many adults, particularly those who indulge in sexist speech. For that reason I am as dubious about the desirability and effectiveness of legalistic measures to deal with this problem as I am about such solutions when dealing with racist speech that is addressed to peers. Sexual harassment statutes or penalties that reach beyond pervasive and persistent patterns of communication, and beyond captive audience situations, to embrace such broad and vague concepts as unwelcome sexual advances are, in my judgment, violative of First Amendment principles. As long as the targets of occasional sexist comments are free to tell the offenders to wise up or get lost and are themselves free to leave the scene if they so choose, the remedy should be, in Justice Brandeis' phrase, "more speech, not enforced silence." It is to the "processes of education," as he suggested, that we should look for the amelioration of sexually insensitive or demeaning interpersonal communication, not to disciplinary committees or law enforcement officials.

Turning to the media of public communication through which sexism may be expressed, one confronts three quite different rationales for the suppression of such speech. The first two of them, in their genesis and primary focus, are not actually concerned with sexism as we understand it today, but with what their advocates see as unhealthy, if not immoral, sexual arousal. It is only incidentally, and of late, that the so-called obscene or pornographic material they would outlaw has also come to be seen as an issue of sexist speech.

The first and most formidable of these positions is that taken for the past half-century by a majority of the Supreme Court, and it is thus the current law of the land. It defines as legally obscene and prohibitable any verbal or pictorial materials that "taken as a whole, appeal to the prurient interest in sex, which portray sexual conduct in a patently offensive way, and which, taken as a whole, do not have serious literary, artistic, political, or scientific value."[2]

Although the justification for this ban has sometimes been based on the assumption that exposure to such words and pictures leads to antisocial sexual conduct, a paucity of reliable empirical evidence supporting that premise has instead caused the proponents of the present restrictions on obscenity to rest their case on its alleged harm to public morality. This rationale was described by former Chief Justice Warren Burger as an "interest of the public in the quality of life and the total community environment."[3] That interest is such a far cry from the kind of direct, immediate, and irreparable harm that the Supreme Court has required before other kinds of speech can be suppressed, that one can only conclude that the obscenity exception to the First Amendment is an anachronistic relic of the Victorian era. A more enlightened Court may some day dispatch it, as the Oregon Supreme Court has already done,[4] to the dustbin of history.

The second approach to the banning of obscene or pornographic communication, on the grounds of its sexual arousal, has enjoyed less popularity than the route taken by the U.S. Supreme Court, but is much more representative of the way in which speech-act thinking has infiltrated this arena of legal discourse. One of its leading advocates is First Amendment scholar Frederick Schauer, who illustrates his position by describing a hypothetical ten-minute film that consists entirely of a close-up color depiction of the sex organs of a male and a female engaged in sexual intercourse. This film, hypothecates Schauer, has "no variety, no dialogue, no music, no artistic depiction."

> The film is shown to paying customers who, observing the film, either reach orgasm instantly or are led to masturbate while the film is being shown. I wish to argue that any definition of "speech"

. . . that included this film in this setting is being bizarrely literal and formalistic. . . . There are virtually no differences in intent and effect from the sale of a plastic or vibrating sex aid, the sale of a body through prostitution, or the sex act itself. . . . [T]he prototypical pornographic item shares more of the characteristics of sexual activity than of communication.[5]

I must risk the charge of being "bizarrely literal and formalistic" by noting the sleight of hand through which Schauer identifies this kind of film as "virtually" no different from prostitution or "the sex act itself." This is the same slippery use of language as comparing fighting words to knocking a chip off someone's shoulder or asserting that a racist slur is like a slap in the face. It totally obliterates the line between representations of reality through words, pictures, or other symbols and reality itself.

It was once wisely observed that "no bull . . . will let its gaze be attracted by a photograph of a cow's rump."[6] Although admittedly we human beings are not bulls and have mental processes that enable us to respond, even physiologically, to representational stimuli, the analogy of a bull's reaction to a picture does make clear an immensely important distinction between symbols and what they represent. It is a vital distinction because it reminds us, again, that the responses of human beings to words, pictures, and other symbols are mediated by their minds; they are not the instinctive and automatic reactions that a bull may have to a cow's rump or, for that matter, that one human may have to another live human.

If Schauer and those who agree with him in believing that obscenity should be illegal were to argue that because human beings, unlike bulls, have the capacity to respond physiologically to verbal and pictorial representations of reality, and that therefore any words or pictures that might lead them to sexual orgasm should be banned, they would be on more solid ground than when they try to erase the boundary line between speech and action. I would still think their position was bizarre, but at least I could not object to it because they had ignored the fundamental difference between symbolic and nonsymbolic behavior.

The third, and newest, rationale for banning pornographic material springs directly and primarily from concerns about its sexist implications and is rooted, like Schauer's position, in speech act theory. Its leading and highly visible spokesperson is Catherine MacKinnon of the University of Michigan School of Law. And it shares much in common with the perspective on racist speech advanced by Charles Lawrence, Mari Matsuda, and others.

Essentially the MacKinnon thesis is that the portrayal of women as demeaned, debased, and abused objects, rather than as persons, in pornographic material is an *act* of subordination, reinforcing and perpetuating a culture of masculine domination and discrimination in which women are the oppressed victims. As such, she argues, pornography should be subject to civil law suits for damages by its targets. Although attempts to write this doctrine into municipal law in Minneapolis and Indianapolis have failed, by mayoral veto in the former and by federal court findings of a violation of the First Amendment in the latter case,[7] the rationale continues to gain attention and sympathy. It has even won the support of the Supreme Court of Canada, which in February of 1992 upheld the obscenity provision of that country's criminal code on the basis of this perspective. Said MacKinnon of that decision, "This makes Canada the first place in the world that says what is obscene is what harms women, not what offends our values. In the United States the obscenity laws are all about not liking to see naked bodies, or homosexual activity, in public. Our laws don't consider the harm to women. But in Canada it will now be materials that subordinate, degrade or dehumanize women that are obscene."[8]

What pleased MacKinnon and her supporters was the Canadian court's assertion that "if true equality between male and female persons is to be achieved, we cannot ignore the threat to equality resulting from exposure to audiences of certain types of violent and degrading material. Materials portraying women as a class as objects for sexual exploitation and abuse have a negative impact on the individual's sense of self-worth and acceptance."[9]

Objections to obscene or pornographic materials that portray women as naturally fair game for abuse and domination are not confined to the media of communication we usually associate with such messages, like X-rated films, peep shows, and so-called adult magazines. Even song lyrics have been called into question—not only the blatantly misogynistic words of groups such as 2 Live Crew, but the more socially acceptable language of traditional college fraternity drinking songs. Two senior women at the University of California at Los Angeles had this to say on the subject:

> A fraternity book of drinking songs that glorifies necrophilia, rape and torture of women is no laughing matter. . . . Phi Kappa Psi President Chris Lee claims that his fraternity's "lyrics are a joke [and] are so exaggerated that it is fairly ridiculous to say these songs promote violence against women." . . . Lee and his supporters refuse to recognize that sexual aggression against women is perpetuated by such institutions as the Greek system. Indeed, victims' descriptions of sexual assault involving fraternity men resemble portrayals of female degradation found in such fraternity songs as "Push Her in a Corner." . . . "Just push her in a corner, and hold her tight like this. Just put your arms around her waist and on her lips a kiss. And if she starts to murmur, or if she starts to cry, just tell her it's the sacred seal of old Phi Kappa Psi." . . .
> Winston Doby, UCLA's vice chancellor, claims that Phi Psi's misogynistic song is protected speech. He is wrong. These "songs" constitute "sexual harassment," prohibited under the state education code, because singing them creates an "intimidating, hostile or offensive . . . educational environment."[10]

Although these women are rightfully alarmed about a culture that spawns such songs as these, they are quite wrong, and their vice chancellor quite right, in their characterizations of this kind of communication. It is, as he asserts, protected speech, and it should be. To invoke the concept of sexual harassment against communicative behavior that is not personally directed in a persistent pattern at particular individuals in a captive audience situation is to stretch that legal terminology far beyond its intended parameters. It opens the door to the suppression of a vast array of speech that may be as benighted, insensitive, emotionally distressing, and reinforcing of socially undesirable attitudes as communication denigrating to racial, religious, and ethnic groups but that, for the same reasons I have presented for hate speech, should not be legally proscribed. As for the MacKinnon view that pornography is an act of sexual subordination that should be subject to legal penalties just as any other act of sex discrimination, the answer is precisely the same as I offered to the argument that racist speech is an act of racial subordination that should be legally prohibited. Speech is not the same as action, and if it were, we would have to scrap the First Amendment.

Still another issue raised by the UCLA women that requires further discussion is their final claim that the Phi Psi song constitutes sexual harassment because it creates an "intimidating, hostile or offensive" environment in violation of the state's education code. This brings me, finally, to the problem that arises in circumstances where interpersonal and public communication may be combined to produce a generally sexist environment. Although such a combination is not true of a fraternity song, which lacks the element of individually targeted communication, it was very much the issue in a difficult and hotly disputed Florida case that merits close attention.

Jacksonville Shiyards is a Florida company that for over a decade has had about half a dozen women working with over eight hundred men. It was common practice for the men to post pictures of nude and partially nude women throughout the workplace and to share pornographic magazines. But beyond this, repeated instances of sexist behavior were directed personally at the women. One female employee complained that whenever she bent over or went up on a ladder some man would yell, "Shoot that thing." A second woman reported that a photograph of a woman's genitals was placed by somebody in her toolbox. A third said that she found obscene comments painted on a jacket she had left on her chair. As one journalist has described it, "Such was the macho shipyard world in which women were treated less like co-workers than as intruders."[11]

After the women's appeals to the company's management about this state of affairs failed to achieve any relief, Lois Robinson, a welder in the shipyard, filed charges of sexual harassment against the company, under Title VII of the federal Civil Rights Act, for allowing and condoning a "hostile work environment." Pursuant to that complaint U.S. District Court Judge Howell Melton found the company liable under the law and ordered them to agree to a sweeping code of prohibited conduct.[12]

In addition to forbidding physical behaviors like "rape, sexual battery, molestation or attempts to commit these assaults," as well as "intentional physical conduct which is sexual in nature, such as touching, pinching, patting, grabbing, brushing against another employee's body, or poking another employee's body," the statement of prohibited conduct included certain types of speech constituting "unwanted sexual advances, propositions or other sexual comments." Among the forbidden were:

(1) sexually-oriented gestures, noises, remarks, jokes, or comments about a person's sexuality or sexual experience directed at or made in the presence of any employee who indicates or has indicated in any way that such conduct in his or her presence is unwelcome.

(2) preferential treatment or promise of preferential treatment to an employee for submitting to sexual conduct, including soliciting or attempting to solicit any employee to engage in sexual activity for compensation or reward; and

(3) subjecting, or threats of subjecting, an employee to unwelcome sexual attention or conduct or intentionally making performance of the employee's job more difficult because of that employee's sex.

Furthermore, the statement prohibited "sexual or discriminatory displays or publications anywhere in JSI's workplace or by JSI employees," including:

(1) displaying pictures, posters, calendars, graffiti, objects, promotional materials, reading materials, or other materials that are sexually suggestive, sexually demeaning, or pornographic, or bringing into the JSI work environment or possessing any such material to read, display or view at work.

A picture will be presumed to be sexually suggestive if it depicts a person of either sex who is not fully clothed or in clothes that are not suited to or ordinarily accepted for the accomplishment of routine work in and around the shipyard and who is posed for the obvious purpose of displaying or drawing attention to private portions of his or her body.

(2) reading or otherwise publicizing in the work environment materials that are in any way sexually revealing, sexually suggestive, sexually demeaning or pornographic. . . .[13]

The company's appeal of the district court's decision to the U.S. Circuit Court of Appeals for the Eleventh Circuit argued that the remedy imposed by the trial judge violated the First Amendment in reaching beyond legitimately prohibitable com-

municative behavior to speech that should be considered constitutionally protected. Robinson's attorneys, on the other hand,
while conceding that pin-up pictures do not by themselves constitute either sexual harassment or a hostile work environment
absent other aggravating circumstances, claimed that the other
circumstances in this case were sufficiently egregious to meet the
sexual harassment test.

The extreme difficulty of drawing the appropriate line between speech that should, and that should not, count as legally
prohibitable sexual harassment is well illustrated by the split
that the Florida case created in the civil liberties and civil rights
communities. Robinson's attorneys were supplied by the National Organization for Women (NOW) Legal Defense and Education Fund. That group's usual ally, the American Civil Liberties
Union (ACLU), came down on the other side, although its Florida
affiliate and national office had some differences of opinion over
how much of the district court's order was unacceptably overbroad. I explain my own view after describing another case that
in many ways is similar to, but in important ways different from,
the Jacksonville Shipyards situation.

The scene in this instance was the Stroh Brewery Company
in St. Paul, Minnesota. The complaint by five women employees
was that a Stroh's television commercial depicting a fictitious
Swedish bikini team descending on an all-male campsite contrib-
uted to the creation of a "hostile work environment" at the
brewery and should therefore be enjoined by the state court in
which they filed suit. The women's lawyers claimed that the
commercial was part of a pattern of behavior allowed by the
company's management that included the use of abusive language and the display of sexually explicit photographs in the
brewery itself; and they claimed that the ad "produces, encour-
ages and condones the [hostile] workshop environment."[14] According to the *Wall Street Journal*, one supporter of the suit, Maria
Angel, a law professor at Temple University, "likens the ads to
those run by an airline company years ago that had female flight
attendants urging customers to 'Fly me.' Had flight attendants
sued, claiming they were harassed on airplanes, Prof. Angel
says, they would have had a strong case. 'I think the ads and
behavior are connected; you can't separate them,' Prof. Angel
says."[15]

This case against Stroh Brewery and the rationale that under-lies it clearly illustrate how the First Amendment may be seri-ously injured as it traverses the minefield of sexual harassment law suits. Professor Angel's assertion that television commercials and sexist acts in the workplace are so intimately connected that "you can't separate them" demonstrates once again how speech-act thinking either blurs the line completely between symbolic and nonsymbolic behavior or, at the least, entices one to believe that exposure to sexist symbols, no matter how distant in time and place from the workshop itself, leads directly and inexorably to sexist conduct in that environment. The inferential leaps re-quired by such reasoning are ones that our legal system has not found acceptable when dealing with other areas of speech, and they should not be accepted with respect to sexist communication even though we are appalled, and rightly so, at the discrimina-tion that women suffer in the workplace.

I do not mean to suggest that the concept of sexual harass-ment in the workplace or, for that matter, in educational and other relatively captive kinds of settings should be thrown out or that there should no limits whatsoever on sexually harassing communication. As I have indicated, I believe that sexist speech can lose its constitutional immunity from punishment *if* there is a persistent pattern of abusive words, gestures, or other symbols directed at specifically targeted individuals in situations from which they cannot, as a practical matter, escape; *if* fair warning has been given that the communication in question is unwelcome and inappropriate; and *if* the effect upon the victims is to interfere demonstrably with their ability to function effectively in that environment. The very same criteria should apply to hate speech based upon the target's race, religion, ethnicity, or sexual orienta-tion, which I would add as a caveat to what was said on that subject in chapter 4.[16]

Although legal remedies may be constitutionally permissi-ble, and perhaps even necessary, for the narrow set of circum-stances just described, they may not be the wisest or most pro-ductive course of action in dealing with the problem of sexism. They do little or nothing to cure the causes of that disease, any more than the banning of racist speech gets rid of group prejudice and hatred. Whether the costs of legalistic measures producing anxiety, uncertainty, and perhaps even resentful backlash in relations between the sexes are worth the benefits of forcefully instructing people on what is unacceptable verbal and symbolic behavior toward members of the opposite sex remains a close question for which I do not have the answer. It is a question, however, that deserves serious consideration.

7

Information and
Communication Theft

In this chapter I am concerned with the kinds of communication that rob people of what is rightfully theirs. These include what in tort law are known as invasions of privacy by the unwanted public disclosure of private facts and by the unauthorized appropriation of a person's name or image for commercial purposes. They also encompass violations of copyright law and the gaining of money or other things of value through fraudulent representations. Such communication comes closer to what might legitimately be called speech acts than anything I can think of and thus presents an arguable exception to the central thesis of this book. I examine each of the examples just mentioned in turn.

With respect to invasions of privacy by unauthorized disclosures of private facts, the basic premise is that one of the most important aspects of personal privacy is the ability to keep certain of one's beliefs and activities to oneself or to restrict the knowledge of those matters to one's most intimate circle. When the press or other people gain access to that knowledge and disseminate it more widely than one desires to have it known, a breach of privacy has occurred. In this respect, privacy is about the control of information. Since the public disclosure of private beliefs and activities through words or pictures is per se a deprivation of that control, an invasion of privacy occurs the moment the information is made public, regardless of who sees it, hears it, reads it, and understands it, and irrespective of what value judgments they make about it. In this sense, the unauthorized and unwanted disclosure of private information might legitimately be considered a speech act.

If I wanted to hold stubbornly and without qualification to my overall thesis regarding speech acts, I might still insist that the act of depriving people of control over private information about themselves is not fully achieved until the disclosure of the words or pictures in question has been followed by somebody else seeing, hearing, or reading, and understanding it. But such an argument would lead to as pointless a semantic dispute as whether there is a sound when a tree falls in the forest and nobody is there to hear it. The fact is there will always be some kind of an audience for a public disclosure of information; otherwise it could not accurately be called public.

The important point is that choosing to label the public disclosure of private information a speech act rather than pure speech does not help at all in deciding whether, or under what circumstances, such speech, or speech acts if one prefers, should be subject to legal restrictions. No one questions the fact that the individual whose privacy has been invaded in this way has been injured, but it is injury of a psychological or emotional sort for which, as I have argued, we must be wary about providing legal remedies. It is for that reason, no doubt, that no provisions in our legal system criminalize the public disclosure of private facts. Rather, the matter has been left to be resolved by civil law suits for damages, when embarrassing private information has been disclosed that, in the view of the particular court hearing the case, is "so intimate and so unwarranted in view of the victim's position as to outrage the community's notions of decency."[1]

The problem of outrageousness as a standard for judicial decision-making was explored in the discussion of hate speech in chapter 4. As I pointed out there, the Supreme Court has deplored the "inherent subjectiveness" of the concept in the context of a public figure's law suit for the intentional infliction of emotional distress. Although the Court has not yet applied that same thinking to suits for the unauthorized and unwanted public disclosure of private facts, I believe the slippery subjectivity of an outrageousness standard is even more apparent in that area. It is instructive to note in this connection how varied over time and place, and over different political and social perspectives, are the notions of what constitute unwarranted and unacceptable invasions of personal privacy.

It was just barely before the turn of this century that invasions of privacy through the communication of information were even recognized as potential candidates for legal redress. The movement to treat such behavior as a tort was given its impetus by two extraordinarily influential articles that appeared in 1890. The first, written by E. L. Godkin, then editor of the *New York*

Evening Post, and published in *Scribner's* magazine, reported on a growing tension between a tendency of the press to cater to the public's curiosity about prominent people's private affairs and the desire of those targets to stay out of the limelight.[2] The second, authored by two distinguished Boston citizens, Samuel D. Warren and Louis D. Brandeis, and published in the prestigious *Harvard Law Review*,[3] was motivated by what they felt to be excessive press coverage of the social life of the Back Bay Warren family and has been described as having "launched a new legal concept which eventually broadened into a principle of information privacy."[4] Thus, twentieth-century American law has extended to the victims of informational hijacking legal remedies that were not available before in Anglo-American jurisprudence.

That which is considered an unwarranted and legally punishable invasion of privacy through communication also varies according to the side of the Atlantic Ocean on which it occurs. In the United States, *Forbes* magazine for many years has published stories identifying America's richest people without anyone giving the matter a second thought. But when a French journal devoted one issue in 1987 to thumbnail sketches of France's hundred richest men,[5] a law suit for invasion of privacy was brought and won by two of them.

One's concept of what should be respected as private is also strongly influenced by one's social and political milieu. William Prosser's landmark law review article explicating the common law tort of invasion of privacy and defending its use of community mores as the benchmark of what is and what is not acceptable, asserted, without so much as a qualifying note, that "the ordinary reasonable man does not take offense at mention in a newspaper of the fact that he has returned from a visit, or gone camping in the woods, or that he has given a party at his house for his friends. . . . It is quite a different matter when the details of sexual relations are spread before the public gaze."[6] It apparently never occurred to Prosser that some people might not want it generally known that they had had a party at their house and that others might very much enjoy having the details of their sex life splashed across the headlines.

A dramatic illustration of how people's political perspectives and agendas can determine what they regard as acceptable public disclosures of private facts occurred during the Persian Gulf War when Pentagon spokesperson Pete Williams gained a great deal of public visibility from the televised press briefings he conducted. At the same time, gay and lesbian activists had become increasingly concerned and vocal about the exclusion of known homosexuals from the armed services. One such group decided that a way to bring pressure on the Pentagon to abandon its exclusionary policy was to "out" Pete Williams—that is, reveal to the public at large what was apparently known to a much smaller circle, that Pete Williams, a close and trusted advisor to the Secretary of Defense, was gay. The effectiveness of this as a political tactic is open to question, and it may well have been viewed by Williams and his associates as an outrageous thing to do. But for those who decided to use the weapon, Pete Williams was apparently regarded as perfectly fair game in their political battle.

Consensus is difficult to achieve not only regarding the outrageousness of particular invasions of privacy through speech, but also as to whether they are justified by their possible newsworthiness. Nevertheless, the courts have consistently accepted claims of newsworthiness as a legitimate defense in invasion of privacy law suits.[7] But what makes a disclosure of information sufficiently newsworthy to outweigh the victim's interest in maintaining privacy? One example of the controversially fine lines that sometimes are drawn in such matters occurred as a result of the explosion of the space shuttle *Challenger* in 1986 that killed the seven astronauts aboard. A tape recording of the astronauts' final words became a matter of considerable interest to the press, which was presumably acting as surrogate for the public in seeking access to arguably newsworthy material. The survivors of those who had perished, however, quite understandably would find a public release of that information to be a painful intrusion on their family privacy. When the National Aeronautics and Space Administration (NASA) came up with the Solomonic compromise of releasing a written transcript of the words on the tape but withholding the actual sound of the voices, that decision was challenged under the Freedom of Information Act by the *New York Times*. The government won that contest in court,[8] but a fair and socially desirable result might just as logically have been achieved by a toss of the coin.

A final puzzle that must be solved when trying to strike a balance between privacy interests, on the one hand, and the public's right to know, on the other, is to determine where, and under what circumstances, people can or should have a reasonable expectation that their privacy will be respected. That is an easy question to answer with respect to what goes on in one's own bedroom or bathroom, or what candidate one selects in a voting booth, or what one says to one's spouse at the dinner table. But what of the unauthorized public dissemination of a photograph of someone kissing one's gay partner on the cheek while standing in a crowd at rush hour waiting for a subway train? Or of a conversation in a restaurant overhead by a reporter at the next table? Or of the information that one has smoked marijuana with a small group of people who were presumed at the time to be trusted friends? Given the modern technology that makes it possible for pictures to be taken and voices to be recorded unobtrusively from great distances, must we assume that our zones of privacy, at least as far as the law is concerned, do not extend beyond the skin that encircles our skulls or the whispers to our spouses in bed? And must we operate on the premise that whenever we divulge our beliefs or expose our actions to anybody else we run the risk that the information may someday, somewhere, appear where we would rather it did not? Those are not very happy or comfortable choices, but understanding what a legal system can and cannot effectively and fairly accomplish leads me to the same conclusion about invasions of privacy through the unwanted disclosure of private facts that I reached years ago:

> E. L. Godkin was right, in that very first essay on privacy in *Scribner's* in 1890, when he doubted that we could look to the law as the best solution for the problem of "mere wounds to feelings." No law that is sensitive to the First Amendment will ever be able to deal appropriately with the aggressive television reporter who aims his camera and sticks his microphone in the face of a sobbing mother who has just learned of the death of all of her children in a fire, and asks her how she feels. As in so many other areas of life, we must rely on the education of the tastes and the elevation of the sensitivities of our citizenry, and on their voluntary respect for the privacy of others, as the remedy most in keeping with the philosophy of a free society.[9]

A second kind of invasion of privacy by communicative behavior that is recognized legally as a tort and that might arguably be considered a speech act, is known as appropriation. It consists of the taking of someone's name or picture without their permission in order to advertise a product or to engage in soe similar commercial usage. Instead of stealing information, as is the case with the unauthorized public disclosure of private facts, what is stolen is the victim's proprietary interest in his or her own name or image and the ability to prevent other people from making a profit on that name or image. The victim's interest is quite similar to that in violations of a copyright. For what is taken without consent when a copyright is breached is not so much the information contained in the plagiarizing publication, which may already have been communicated to the public in other forms, but rather the particular manner, style, words, or pictures used by the original copyright holder.

With both appropriation and copyright violations, damage to the proprietary interests of the victim is done the instant the communication in question is seen or heard by others. To put it another way, the theft has been accomplished in that moment. Thus it is possibly appropriate to label this a speech act. But just as with the unauthorized disclosure of private facts, the label one attaches to these phenomena is not much help in determining whether legal restrictions should be invoked. Whether copyright violations and appropriation of names or images are regarded as speech acts or as pure speech, the injury they do to tangible assets of the victim is sufficiently great, and the free speech interest of the robber sufficiently slight, to justify the invocation of social controls through the law.

Rodney Smolla, in his recent volume on freedom of speech,[10] has classified the foregoing kinds of communicative behavior, plus fraud, false advertising, and personal libel, into a category that he describes as doing "relational harm." He sets this in contrast to the "physical harm" done by acts of violence and to what he calls the "reactive harm" done by hate speech and other communication that creates emotional distress for its targets. He agrees with me and many others that the infliction of physical harm should be punishable by the law and that the infliction of emotional distress should not be. But he parts company from me in arguing that *all* speech that produces so-called relational harms should fall within the purview of the law. He includes under this rubric communication that interferes with "social relationships, commercial transactions, proprietary interests in information, and interests in the confidentiality of communications."[11]

I would make distinctions among the forms of communicative behavior that Smolla has lumped together as causing relational harm and would subject only some of them to legal restrictions. Also, I would do so for reasons different from those advanced by Smolla. My touchstone is how close each of them comes to being an accomplished act of theft by virtue of its mere utterance, publication, or dissemination. That test is most clearly met by two of the three types of communication Smolla lists in his relational harms subcategory of "injuries to information ownership," that is, copyright violations and appropriations of names or images for commercial purposes. But he also includes in this subcategory the unauthorized public disclosure of private facts that, I would argue, are problematic more because of the emotional distress they produce than because of any theft of the victim's palpable assets. Hence, I would separate the public disclosure of private facts from copyright violations and appropriations, reluctantly exempting the former from legal remedies and reserving such sanctions for the latter.

With respect to libel and slander, which Smolla places in a subcategory of relational harm that he labels "injuries to social relationships," and with respect to fraud and false advertising, which he classifies as "injuries to transactions or business relationships," I would maintain that because such communication causes injury only if believed and acted upon, it does not per se constitute a theft in the same way as copyright violations or appropriations do. If there is time, opportunity, and a source from which corrective information may be disseminated to those who have been the audience for false claims, those falsehoods may do no harm at all. They are accomplished speech acts only if such intervening variables are not, or cannot be, introduced before the audience or victim takes action based upon the false representations that have been made. It is instructive to note in this connection that common law actions for the tort of "deceit" have traditionally required that before one can recover damages in such a law suit there must be proof that there has been "reliance upon the representation on the part of the plaintiff, in taking action or refraining from it," and that there has been "damage to the plaintiff, resulting from such reliance."[12]

I recognize that it is not always feasible to follow the admonition of Justice Brandeis, that "if there be time to expose through discussion the falsehood and fallacies, to avert the evil by the processes of education, the remedy to be applied is more speech, not enforced silence." There may be no time to answer libelous charges against a candidate for public office on the eve of an election before voters go to their polling places. There may be no agencies, public or private, with the resources to test the veracity of all the product advertising that is communicated to the public or to disseminate what information they manage to obtain to as wide an audience as was exposed to the original false claims. There may be no practical way to warn all gullible victims against the frauds that con artists seem ever ready to perpetrate against them before parting with their money or worldly goods.

For all these pragmatic reasons it may be necessary to have recourse to social controls through the law to prevent, insofar as possible, and to punish where prevention has failed, the theft of palpable assets that may result from the communication of falsehoods. But we should recognize, as we do this, that in the best of all possible worlds these potential thefts would be prevented in the first place by the Brandeis remedy of "more speech, not enforced silence."

8

Victimless
Communicative
Actions

In the earlier chapters of this book, I have repeatedly insisted that a significant boundary must be respected between the pure speech or expression of words, pictures, and nonverbal symbols, on the one hand, and nonsymbolic conduct that has physical consequences but possibly also communicative purposes, on the other hand. I have argued, with respect to the former, that the First Amendment is always implicated, although it need not always triumph over other competing interests. With regard to the latter, I have suggested a further important distinction. Some acts such as assassinations and hate crimes may have as one of their purposes, if not their primary purpose, the sending of a political or social message to the world, but are so clearly and palpably injurious to others that no claim to First Amendment protection can be seriously entertained.

Other acts, however, that may sometimes be engaged in for communicative purposes, like the burning of a draft card or sleeping in a park where camping is prohibited, have physical consequences that are not directly or seriously harmful to other people and might thus be called victimless crimes. Whether there is literally such a thing as a victimless crime is a debatable proposition, since it can be argued that much conduct often claimed to be victimless, such as suicide, polygamy, excessive drinking, or indulging in other drugs, may in fact significantly and adversely affect the lives of others, directly or indirectly.

Yet there are clearly some behaviors that society, for moral or pragmatic reasons, and for good or bad reasons, has decided to make illegal—like public nudity, certain kinds of sexual behavior between consenting adults, public burning of a draft card, or sleeping in parks not designated for that purpose—whose physical consequences for other persons or for society in general are so minimal, inconsequential, or even nonexistent that the so-called offense is, for all practical purposes, victimless. When such conduct is engaged in for communicative purposes, then a claim for First Amendment protection deserves serious contemplation, and that is what I intend to do in this chapter.

My position is apparently shared to some extent by the Supreme Court. Although in *U.S. v. O'Brien* it declared that "we cannot accept the view that an apparently limitless variety of conduct can be labelled 'speech' whenever the person engaging in the conduct intends thereby to express an idea," the Court then proceeded to hold that "when 'speech' and 'nonspeech' elements are combined in the same course of conduct" the non-speech elements may be regulated *only* if the regulation "furthers an important or substantial government interest; if the govern-mental interest is unrelated to the suppression of free expression; and if the incidental restriction on alleged First Amendment freedom is no greater than is essential to the furtherance of that interest."[1]

Like the dissenters in the Supreme Court's later decision on sleeping in the park (discussed below), I find these criteria reasonable and useful for adjudicating victimless communicative actions. But I question, as they did, the manner in which those standards were applied by the Court's majority in that case. I question even more critically the way they were applied in the *O'Brien* case itself.

In *O'Brien*, the majority found that there was a substantial government interest unrelated to the suppression of free expres-sion in the Selective Service System's need to efficiently maintain and effectively enforce the draft by prohibiting registrants from destroying their certificates of registration (i.e., their draft cards) and by requiring them to keep the cards in their possession at all times. But this position was seriously flawed. If the concern of the Selective Service System was that draft card burners were trying to evade the draft by destroying the evidence of their registration, that would be a thin reed on which to lean. Burning a draft card did not obliterate the registrant's file at his draft board's office, and destroying the card at a public rally would hardly be the best way to escape the draft board's notice. If the purpose of requiring possession of one's draft card at all times was so that spot checks could be made of young men to see if they had registered for the draft as they were supposed to have done—an activity the government did not, in fact, engage in—that goal was already met by a provision of the original Selective Service Act requiring such possession. It was not aided in any way by the redundant amendment later adopted by the Congrss specifically banning public draft card burning, the provision of the law that was invoked against O'Brien and other offenders. Had these men simply been charged with nonpossession of their cards, which obviously would have been their situation after burning the cards, their claim to First Amendment protection would have been more tenuous. Being charged with violating the draft card burning amendment made that claim much more viable.

Indeed, the most glaring defect in the Supreme Court's rationale was its contention that the congressional amendment to the Selective Service Act prohibiting public draft card burning, and the prosecutions pursuant to it, were "unrelated to the suppression of free expression." If that were true the amendment would have been unnecessary, for nonpossession was already illegal before its passage. And to anyone who read the record of the congressional debate preceding adoption of the amendment, it was clear that the law was motivated by, and designed to punish, those who were expressing their opposition to the Vietnam War by publicly burning their draft cards. The Court majority simply closed its eyes to that fact by asserting that it was not the proper role of the Court to read the minds of the legislators who voted for the bill, but to judge it only on its face. From that perspective the majority concluded that it was a content-neutral ban on pure conduct that had nothing to do with freedom of speech. If one believes that, one will believe anything.

The decision the Supreme Court had to make sixteen years later in the case of a demonstration against homelessness in Lafayette Park across from the White House was, in my opinion, a much closer call than it had been with respect to draft card burning, though by no means was it the frivolous issue that then Chief Justice Warren Burger said it was.[2] The protesting group wanted to set up camp in Lafayette Park to symbolize the fact that many people had no place else to sleep and to urge the government to do more about the problem of homelessness. National Park Service rules permit such camping in other District of Columbia parks but not in this one. The rules do allow demonstrations to take place in Lafayette Park and even allow structures such as tents to be erected as part of those demonstrations, but do not permit sleeping in them. When the protesters were denied an exception to this rule they challenged that decision in court, claiming a denial of their First Amendment right to communicate their message through sleeping. They succeeded in persuading a majority of the U.S. Circuit Court of Appeals for the District of Columbia of the merit of this argument,[3] but that decision was overturned by a 7–2 vote of the Supreme Court.[4]

Applying the *O'Brien* criteria, the Supreme Court majority quite reasonably concluded that there was an important government interest in excluding camping from Lafayette Park, that the rule against it had been applied in a content-neutral manner to all groups without discrimination, that it was unrelated in its purpose to the suppression of free expression, and that it was no broader than necessary to preserve the park for the uses for which it was intended.

Justice Thurgood Marshall, writing a dissenting opinion for himself and Justice Brennan, found no fault with the *O'Brien* criteria but felt that, in applying them, the majority had given too much weight to the government's interest in limiting the uses of the park and too little weight to the protesting group's free speech interest in communicating a message symbolically by sleeping. He did not contend that the rule against camping, as it might generally be applied, was itself in violation of the First Amendment, but only that the First Amendment required an exception to be made for camping as expressive behavior.[5]

The majority and dissenting arguments in this case are ones about which reasonable people can legitimately differ. The government's interest looks quite flimsy when, as Justice Marshall pointed out, the Park Service suggested that the protesters could, if they wished, *pretend* to sleep, but could not actually do so.[6] On the other hand, if the dissenters' position were adopted, the authorities and courts would have to get into the risky business of deciding who is entitled to an exception to a rule directed at pure conduct because they claim that the purpose of that conduct is to send a message to the world.

Those two issues are at the core of the more general problem of whether, or to what extent, *any* victimless but still illegal communicative action should be given First Amendment protection. How substantial is the government's interest in preventing or punishing the behavior in question? And what are the implications of making an exception to a law that governs ordinarily prohibitable conduct because that conduct is being used in the particular instance for communicative purposes?

For Supreme Court Justice Antonin Scalia, there is a clear and simple answer to these questions. If his view were to prevail, it would be virtually impossible for any victimless communicative act to win First Amendment protection. I explore his point of view as representative of the most extreme position on this matter and as the one to which I take the sharpest exception.

The first and most forceful articulation in a Supreme Court opinion of the Scalia perspective came not in a First Amendment freedom of speech case but in a First Amendment free exercise of religion case.[7] Yet the principles he enunciated can be applied to both, and Justice Scalia did, in fact, take precisely the same approach in a freedom of speech case the following year.[8] The free exercise of religion case involved a claim by native Americans who use peyote as part of their religious ceremony that the State of Oregon's denial of unemployment benefits to them for disobeying the state's drug law violated their First Amendent right to the free exercise of religion. A six-person majority of the Supreme Court rejected that claim, with Justice Scalia writing the majority opinion on behalf of himself and four others.

The essence of that opinion was that a law of general applicability that is within the legitimate sphere of government authority and is not designed particularly to violate anyone's First Amendment rights may be enforced uniformly and without exception, even if that enforcement has the incidental effect of curbing a religious activity. Justice Scalia and his colleagues felt that the Oregon statute prohibiting the use of peyote was a perfectly reasonable law, entirely within the legislative authority of the state, and that if it had the effect in this particular instance of inhibiting someone's religious activity, that was just their misfortune. Their relief, if they wanted it, suggested Justice Scalia, was through the political process, where they could try to persuade a majority of the legislature to make an exception for them (which has been done in some states) or to scrap the law altogether. Recourse was not to be found in the First Amendment.

Justice Sandra Day O'Connor agreed with the Court's decision that in this particular case the state's interest in prohibiting drug abuse outweighed the native American freedom of religion claim. However, she was so appalled at the route taken by Justice Scalia to arrive at his conclusion that she wrote a separate concurring opinion that reads more like a dissent.[9] Indeed, the three actual dissenters agreed entirely with the rationale of her opinion and parted company from her only as to the conclusion she reached from those premises. She put her finger directly on what I agree is the great danger of the Scalia point of view. In that view, Justice O'Connor points out, the First Amendment, instead of being the protection for minority rights against majority will that its authors had in mind, is abandoned in favor of a majoritarian concept of governance. The Constitution thus gives no protection to minorities beyond what a legislative majority is willing to grant, and the courts have no role in, nor basis for, overriding those legislative judgments. In other words, when religious *activities* rather than mere beliefs are at issue, there might as well not be a First Amendment, as far as a majority of the Supreme Court was concerned.

If there were any doubt about it, the implications of Justice Scalia's point of view for the freedom of speech provision of the First Amendment became entirely clear a year after the peyote decision when the Supreme Court decided that an Indiana law prohibiting nude dancing in bars did not violate the First Amendment.[10] But this time the vote was only 5–4, and the five-person majority was split three different ways in its reasons for upholding the restriction. A plurality opinion, written by Chief Justice William Rehnquist for himself and Justices O'Connor and Kennedy, followed essentially the same approach with respect to this free speech claim as Justice O'Connor had taken with respect to the freedom of religion claim in the peyote case and as the Court's majority had taken in the Lafayette Park case. In brief, the three justices took the position that dancing is a form of expression entitled to First Amendment consideration, but that sine dancing in the nude involves both speech and nonspeech elements, the *O'Brien* criteria were the tests to be applied to determine if the First Amendment should prevail. Applying those standards, they concluded that the government had a legitimate public morality interest in banning nudity in public places that was unrelated to the suppression of free expression.

As with the ban on sleeping in Lafayette Park, they believed that the limitation on expression in this instance was so minimal and incidental that it passed constitutional muster.[11]

Justice David Souter, in a separate concurring opinion, agreed with both the plurality and the dissenters that the *O'Brien* criteria were the appropriate tests and agreed further with the plurality that those tests had been met. But his reasons for that were somewhat different. He believed that the government interest that justified the ban on public nudity as applied to dancing in bars was not society's "moral views" regarding nudity, but rather its interest in preventing the prostitution, sexual assault, criminal activity, and other harmful "secondary effects" that are associated with adult entertainment establishments such as these bars.[12]

Souter also felt it useful and important to make a distinction between what he called "performance dancing" and dancing in general. He described the former as "inherently expressive," whereas the latter may or may not be.[13] In this case, where the dancing was plainly a performance, he believed that the First Amendment clearly applied. But that did not mean that it prevailed. For here it was combined with nudity, which made it a different story. Since, in Souter's view, the state had a valid interest in prohibiting nudity in bars—an interest unrelated to the suppression of freedom of speech—the *O'Brien* tests were passed.

The four dissenters also used the *O'Brien* standards as their measuring rod but came to an opposite conclusion.[14] The government interest in prohibiting nude dancing in bars, they asserted, was not to protect the public from any real harm but to stop what the state believed to be "the harmful message that nude dancing communicates." Thus their purpose was not unrelated, but was directly related, to the suppression of free expression. It failed that *O'Brien* criterion, they said, in the very same way that the Court had found laws against flag burning to fail the criterion.

Happily, Justice Scalia was the odd man out in the nude dancing decision. His separate concurring opinion agreed only with the majority's final judgment that the Indiana law should be upheld, but he invoked as its rationale the very same argument he had made with respect to peyote. The Indiana ban on public nudity was a law of general applicability, regulating conduct and not specifically directed at expression. It was, therefore, in his view, not subject to First Amendment scrutiny at all. If a society's majority, in its wisdom, makes a reasonable judgment that public nudity should be prohibited, the fact that somebody wants to use nudity as a means of communicating a message, even as part of a stage performance, does not entitle that activity to First Amendment consideration.[15]

Justice Scalia elaborated his perspective on these matters during the course of a televised discussion of "The First Amendment and Hate Speech" carried by the Public Broadcasting System on 11 February, 1992. He illustrated his point with the difference between a hypothetical law that would ban putting one's arm out of a car window to shake a fist at someone else and another hypothetical law banning all putting of arms out of car windows. The former, like laws against flag burning, he said, would violate the First Amendment because its direct and sole purpose would be the suppression of free expression. The latter, however, even if applied to someone who shook a fist out of a car window at somebody else, would be entirely permissible, because it would be a law of general applicability aimed at conduct and not speech and thus would be of no relevance to the First Amendment.

This illustration, although given off-the-cuff, reveals another danger of the Scalia perspective beyond its frightening majoritarian implications noted by Justice O'Connor in her peyote opinion. Although in his court opinions Justice Scalia has qualified what the majority may do in regulating conduct by saying that it must have a rational basis, it is difficult to discern what, if anything, in the way of majority rule over behavior other than pure speech he would ever regard as irrational. If a law against people putting their arms out of their car windows is an example of reasonable majority decision-making, one cannot help but wonder what kind of Big Brother society Justice Scalia might find constitutionally acceptable.[16]

This brings me to an issue that transcends freedom of speech concerns, although it has serious ramifications for those concerns as well. It is the tendency of society, or more accurately its legislators who presumably represent social attitudes, to restrict certain kinds of behavior, not because of any harmful physical consequences they may have for others, but because they are behaviors considered by many or most people to be aesthetically offensive, morally repugnant, or self-destructive to the persons engaging in them. I have more to say about this matter in the next chapter, but it needs to be considered here because many, although not all, of the First Amendment dilemmas posed by victimless communicative actions would be eliminated if society were to refrain from prohibiting such conduct, whether or not it is used for communicative or religious purposes. That would be true of everything, for example, from the private possession and use of drugs, to sexual intercourse in public, to public nudity, to sodomy (in private or in public), to dress codes in the public schools.

But what shall we do about victimless communicative actions in the present, real world where such behaviors are not about to be generally permitted? When should exceptions be made to nondiscriminatory, content-neutral laws of general applicability because, in particular instances, the behavior is being used for communicative purposes? One potentially useful answer may be found in Justice Souter's distinction between performance dancing and dancing in general. That distinction can be extended to other behaviors like public nudity, where someone might engage in it offstage just because it feels enjoyable, but does it onstage as part of an artistic message. Why not make a broad exception to laws of general applicability directed at victimless offenses, when those actions are part of a performance on a stage or screen?

Another distinction I propose is between actions such as how, or how much, one dresses or undresses, wears one's hair, or shaves, on the one hand, and actions such as urination, defecation, and expectoration, on the other hand. The former set of actions might be motivated entirely by considerations of physical comfort or self-satisfaction, or entirely by intent to communicate particular messages to the world (and thus would be purely symbolic behavior), or by some combination thereof. Whatever the case might be, since they have no physical consequences for others, it is difficult to see the justification for any restrictions upon them. To be sure, some exceptional considerations, such as avoiding having students in a public school distracted from their work by classmates appearing at school in the nude, might justify narrow restrictions on personal appearance. But there was no such justification, in my view, for school officials in an Oklahoma community to tell Pawnee Indian children that in order to stay in school they must cut off their long braids—a clearly symbolic expression of the culture and customs of those children and their families. Astonishingly, the federal courts upheld the authority of the public school officials in that case.[17]

If, on the other hand, the actions involve urination, defecation, or expectoration, and they are not done in appropriate places, they do have physical consequences for others, whether engaged in solely to relieve oneself, as is usually the case, or, in rare instances, directed at other people or at inappropriate locations for the purpose of communicating disrespect or hostility. Whichever may be the case, society is justified in prohibiting the behavior without exceptions. Thus, if people spit upon political candidates because they do not like their views, which has happened, or if someone dumps a pile of feces in a city hall lobby to protest a mayor's inaction in enforcing a public nuisance ordinance, which has also happened, a claim of First Amendment protection for the behavior should not be taken seriously. I see no difference in principle, though certainly there are differences in the degree of injury to others, between those actions and painting political slogans on somebody else's building, burning a cross on someone else's front lawn, burning down their house, or committing an assassination.

If one comes to the conclusion, as I do, that there are some relatively victimless offenses that society may legitimately proscribe, like attending a public school in the nude, or that society is going to proscribe, whether we like it or not, but that, if they cause no real harm to other people, exceptions to the prohibition should be made when the action is undertaken for communicative purposes, then one must come to terms with the problem of potentially unfair discrimination in who gets First Amendment protection and who does not. If demonstrators for homelessness are allowed to sleep in Lafayette Park, why should not the Boy Scouts? And what if the Boy Scouts claim, perhaps sincerely and perhaps not, that the reason they want to camp there instead of some place else is to persuade the White House that the government should not interfere with the exclusion of atheists from their organization? If native Americans are allowed to use generally prohibited drugs as part of their religious ceremony, what happens if somebody else who wants to use drugs claims that he or she has established a church in which the use of drugs is a ceremonial requirement, as Timothy Leary did a number of years ago?

Justice Marshall's answer, in his dissent from the Supreme Court's decision on sleeping in the park, was that there is nothing unusual about government agencies or courts engaging in "the delicate task of inquiring into the sincerity of claimants asserting First Amendment rights." He cites as an example the religious exemption from compulsory school attendance laws the Court gave to the Amish.[18] One could also cite the delicate task the government engages in when it inquires into the sincerity and depth of conviction of those who seek conscientious objector status in order to be excused from military combat service.

I am not sure that this is an entirely satisfactory answer, either for religious exemptions to generally applicable laws or for exemptions based on claims that the activity is undertaken in order to communicate a political, social, or artistic message. There is a serious potential for abuse by claimants and for misjudgments by the government and the courts, perhaps even more so with respect to free speech claims than with freedom of religion claims. But so long as the exceptions are limited, as they must be, to the kinds of behavior whose physical consequences for others are minimal, inconsequential, or nonexistent, no great harm will be done, even if occasional mistakes are made in a permissive direction. It is a small risk to take and a small price to pay to maintain a robust First Amendment.

9

Morality and
the Law

We sometimes hear it said, "you can't legislate morality." That assertion is a vast oversimplification of a complicated subject. We do legislate morality on many matters, with murder, rape, robbery, and child abuse being just a few examples. We also refrain from invoking the law, in many circumstances, against other behaviors that large numbers of people regard as immoral, such as lying, breaking promises, and adultery. And then there is an issue like abortion, which large numbers of our citizens fervently feel should be illegal, and even larger numbers strongly believe should be a matter of personal choice.

There seems to be a broad consensus that what people *think*, even if it is immoral, is not an appropriate matter for control by the law and that, for the most part, they should also be allowed to *say* what they think. But speech act theory has begun to erode the latter half of that consensus. By defining certain kinds of arguably immoral symbolic behavior, such as hate speech, pornography, or portrayals of violence, as acts rather than pure speech, speech-act advocates make it much easier to sell the argument that such conduct should be subject to social control through the law. For the closer those behaviors regarded as immoral come to having identifiably harmful consequences for others—which acts are more likely to have than pure speech—the stronger becomes the case for making them illegal.

A graphic example of how this line of thought plays out is a law review article by Lawrence Solum published in 1989.[1] Solum constructs his thesis on the foundations of the speech act theory of Jurgen Habermas, a German philosopher of language who advocates communication that he describes as nonstrategic and nonmanipulative and that is thus conducive to what he calls an "ideal speech situation."[2] Although Habermas himself does not go this far, Solum argues that any speech that does not fall within the Habermasian domain of rational discourse, speech that Habermas calls "strategic action," should not be immune from legal sanctions. "Strategic action," writes Solum, "is, in theory, beyond the protection of the first amendment, even if the danger it poses is fuzzy and remote."[3]

Solum is on solid ground insofar as some of the speech that Habermas classifies as strategic action, such as coercive and deceptive communication, is, in particular circumstances, already considered by our courts to be outside the boundaries of the First Amendment. I noted earlier that that is the case with respect to direct verbal threats of physical harm, and it is also the situation, for example, with regard to fraud in commercial transactions. But there is also much irrational persuasion that goes on in our world that would fail the Habermas tests of ideal speech, but that no one has seriously contended should be unprotected by the First Amendment. Were it otherwise, there would have to be a massive overhaul of current practices of political campaigning and commercial advertising. Although highly desirable from an ethical or moral point of view, the idea that Habermasian standards might be enforced on our election campaigns by the police and the courts is frightening to contemplate. That would surely be "political correctness" run amok.

Rejecting the extreme position taken by Solum still leaves the question where we *should* draw the line against writing morality into law, whether with respect to purely physical behaviors, purely symbolic conduct, or combinations of the two. To that question, I propose the following. The first criterion is that before a moral standard concerning a particular behavior is codified into law, there should be a near-unanimous consensus in society that the conduct in question is indeed immoral. That is why we have no problem with laws against murder, rape, robbery, or child abuse, for even those who commit those offenses, unless they are insane, would concede that the actions are wrong. On the other hand, one reason, although perhaps not the primary reason, for not outlawing all adultery, lying, or breaking of promises, is that many people, even if they may not publicly admit it, do not regard those behaviors as immoral, or at least not immoral under all circumstances.

The reason that abortion creates such a dilemma is that those who believe it should be outlawed equate it with murder which, in their view, everyone should agree is unacceptable in a civilized society. And, indeed, if everyone, or nearly everyone, believed that abortion is the same as murder there would be no problem with its being outlawed. But the fact is they do not. A majority of people see a difference between abortion and murder, and although many still regard abortion as something they would not choose for themselves, they recognize that this is a moral judgment about which individuals differ. When there is such an absence of societal consensus about the morality of a particular act, to outlaw that behavior is to impose the moral judgment of some upon the moral judgment of others and, in this case, that of an apparent minority upon an apparent majority. But even if it were the other way around, with perhaps as much as a two-thirds majority believing abortion to be murder, that would still not make the imposition of their moral judgment through law legitimate.

I am well aware that an anti-abortion advocate would respond that by *not* outlawing abortion we impose the moral judgment of the pro-choice forces on those who disagree with them and, in so doing, put society in the position of condoning murder. But that assumes, once again, that abortion is murder, and that is the very premise that is in contention. A free society simply cannot function as such if moral premises that are not almost universally agreed to are written into the law.

Although it is not a speech issue, I have used abortion to explain my views because that topic so clearly highlights the considerations that also dictate my position with respect to communicative behavior. Even though a majority might wish it were so, there is clearly no consensus in our society that so-called obscene or pornographic material is immoral. There may be a broader consensus with respect to the general idea of expression that denigrates people on the basis of their race or religion, but when one gets down to particulars, like the telling of an ethnic joke to one's friends, or the unthinking utterance of a racial epithet in anger or frustration, that moral consensus soon disintegrates.

I have heard students in my classes on the ethics of communication disagree vehemently over the circumstances under which so-called white lies are, if ever, unethical; and similarly disagree about the use of sexual appeals or celebrity testimonials in commercial advertising, the ghost writing of speeches, thirty-second TV political ads, and the unauthorized publication of the names of rape victims. These are all issues of significant and serious moral concern, but in part because of a lack of societal consensus about them, they are not appropriate subjects for social control by law.

But a lack of societal consensus is not the only reason for staying the hand of the law when dealing with morally problematic expressive behavior. Laws, to be credible and fair, must be practically enforceable and the authorities must not be quixotic in applying them. Yet our experience with most regulations of allegedly immoral speech through law enforcement has demonstrated that they usually run afoul of one or both of these criteria.

How, for example, can laws or school disciplinary codes against hate speech reach every racist or sexist utterance that occurs, and who will be selected as the targets for the necessarily occasional enforcement? It is noteworthy that in an inordinate number of the cases in which campus speech codes designed to protect minorities from verbal abuse have been invoked, they have been used against the members of minority groups themselves for utterances they directed at others. It is instructive, furthermore, to note how obscenity prosecutions tend to increase when the law enforcement official in charge of them is running for reelection and how they get put on the back burner at other times. They also tend to be directed at the most highly visible targets, such as performers like 2 Live Crew or an artist like Robert Mapplethorpe, much more than at run-of-the-mill alleged offenders.

A prime example of an unenforced, and probably unenforceable, law restricting communication that could only be enforced, if at all, on a sporadic and arbitrary basis was, nevertheless, upheld by the Supreme Court in 1981.[4] It happens to be a law not against something immoral, but rather against the depositing of unstamped material in people's mailboxes. Yet it vividly illustrates the point I am making about laws directed at allegedly immoral speech. A majority of the Supreme Court rejected the claim by a civic association in the town of Greenburgh, New York, that the federal prohibition against the inexpensive door-to-door distribution of their meeting notices in neighbors' mailboxes constituted a violation of their First Amendment rights. Mailboxes are not a public forum, said the Court, and the postal service's interest in reserving them for paying customers was a legitimate, content-neutral concern. But Justice Stevens, in his dissenting opinion, made the statement that is relevant here. "Finally," he said, enumerating his reasons for believing that the law should be struck down, "we should not ignore the fact that nobody has ever been convicted of violating this middle-aged nationwide statute. It must have been violated literally millions of times."[5]

I come, finally, to the criterion that ultimately marks the difference between a free society and a totalitarian or theocratic one. It is the test articulated a century and a half ago in John Stuart Mill's essay *On Liberty* to which I have had recourse throughout this book: What harm does the behavior in question do to other people? That is, as I have shown, often not a simple question to answer, for there are various degrees of seriousness of harm to others that one's conduct can cause: the harm can be direct and immediate or indirect and remote; and the injury can be more psychological than physical, though, as Freud and others have long since shown us, the former can sometimes lead to the latter.

A free society will always draw the line between what it considers immoral and what it makes illegal as close as possible to the more serious, direct, immediate, and physical of the harms, and it will leave to the operations of social pressure, education, and self-restraint the control of behaviors whose harm to others is less serious, less direct, less immediate, and less physical. Totalitarian or theocratic societies will do just the opposite, for they make no distinction between morality and law. They think they know for certain what is good and what is bad for people, in both the short run and the long run, both physically and emotionally, and do not hesitate to write those judgments into law.

A free society, by contrast, does not regard the moral judgments of either its majority or its political and religious leaders as infallible. Hence it refrains from coercive measures to enforce them, except where that is necessary to insure that the exercise of one person's freedom and autonomy does not clearly and demonstrably interfere with the freedom and autonomy of others. It is because words, pictures, and other symbolic behaviors are, by their very nature, far less likely than physically consequential conduct to reach that level of harmfulness, that we must preserve, in our minds and the minds of those who make and administer our laws, the distinction between speech and action. I believe that the blurring of that line through speech-act thinking leads down the road to an intermingling of morality and the law that can be the undoing of a free society.

Notes
Index

Notes

1. Introduction

1. "Student at Brown is Expelled under a Rule Barring 'Hate Speech'," *New York Times*, 12 Feb. 1991, A 17.

2. Critics did not claim that Brown, as a private rather than state university, was legally bound by the strictures of the First Amendment, nor was Gregorian conceding that it was. The issue was one of appropriate policy for an institution of higher education. Both Brown and its critics were operating on a premise, articulated in President Gregorian's letter, that "freedom-of-speech questions lie at the heart of any academic community" and that "imposed orthodoxies of all sorts, including what is called 'politically correct' speech, are anathema to our enterprise" (Letter to the Editor, *New York Times*, 21 Feb. 1991, A 20).

3. Thomas Emerson, *The System of Freedom of Expression* (New York: Random House, 1970); Frederick Schauer, *Free Speech: A Philosophical Enquiry* (New York: Cambridge University Press, 1982).

4. Schauer, *Free Speech*, 50–52.

5. Stanley Fish, "There's No Such Thing as Free Speech and It's a Good Thing Too," *Boston Review*, Feb. 1992, 23.

6. *Chaplinsky v. New Hampshire*, 315 U.S. 568 (1942) at 572.

7. *Chaplinsky*, 315 U.S. at 572.

8. Schauer, *Free Speech*, 181.

9. See, for example, Catherine MacKinnon, *Feminism Unmodified: Discourses on Life and Law* (Cambridge: Harvard University Press, 1987), and Andrea Dworkin, *Pornography: Men Possessing Women* (New York: Dutton, 1981).

10. Paul Brest and Ann Vandenberg, "Politics, Feminism, and the Constitution: The Anti-Pornography Movement in Minneapolis," *Stanford Law Review* 39 (1987): 659, summarizing the position taken by Catherine MacKinnon and Andrea Dworkin.

11. Mari Matsuda, "Public Response to Racist Speech: Considering the Victim's Story," *Michigan Law Review* 87 (1988): 2358. See also, for this point of view, Charles R. Lawrence, III, "If He Hollers Let Him Go: Regulating Racist Speech on Campus," *Duke Law Journal* 1990: 431–83.

12. Kent Greenawalt, *Speech, Crime, and the Uses of Language* (New York: Oxford University Press, 1989), 58.

13. Harry Kalven, Jr., "The Concept of the Public Forum: Cox v.

Louisiana," *Supreme Court Review* (Chicago: University of Chicago Press, 1965), 23.

14. Alexander Meiklejohn, one of the earliest so-called First Amendment absolutists, provided an example of such regulations in his classic work, *Free Speech and Its Relation to Self Government* (New York: Harper and Brothers, 1948), a volume that was later republished in an expanded form and entitled *Political Freedom* (New York: Harper and Brothers, 1960). Using a New England town meeting as his analogy, he pointed out that operating such a meeting according to Roberts' Rules of Order, which assure, for instance, that two people do not talk at the same time, are the kinds of neutral limitations on speech that are not only permissible but necessary to insure that everyone gets a fair chance to be heard.

15. Emerson had first described these four values in a law review article that was, with some modification, republished as a book entitled *Toward a General Theory of the First Amendment* (New York: Random House, 1966). He then incorporated those values into the first chapter of his major work, *The System of Freedom of Expression*.

16. Meiklejohn, *Free Speech*.

17. Martin Redish, *Freedom of Expression: A Critical Analysis* (Charlottesville, VA: Michie Co., 1984); C. Edwin Baker, *Human Liberty and Freedom of Speech* (New York: Oxford University Press, 1989).

18. Vincent Blasi, "The Checking Value in First Amendment Theory," *American Bar Foundation Research Journal* (Chicago: American Bar Foundation, 1977), 521–649.

19. Schauer, *Free Speech*, 86.

20. Lee Bollinger, *The Tolerant Society* (New York: Oxford University Press, 1986).

21. Paul Chevigny, *More Speech: Dialogue Rights and Modern Liberty* (Philadelphia: Temple University Press, 1987); Steven Shiffrin, *The First Amendment, Democracy, and Romance* (Cambridge: Harvard University Press, 1990).

2. Situation-Altering Utterances

1. Ludwig Wittgenstein, *Culture and Value*, ed. P. Winch (Chicago: University of Chicago Press, 1980), 46e.

2. J. L. Austin, *How to Do Things with Words* (Cambridge: Harvard University Press, 1962), and "Performative Utterances," in *Philosophical Papers*, 3d ed. (London: Oxford University Press, 1979), 233–52; John R. Searle, *Speech Acts: An Essay in the Philosophy of Language* (London: Cambridge University Press, 1969), and "A Taxonomy of Illocutionary Acts," in *Language, Mind and Knowledge*, ed. Keith Gunderson (Minneapolis: University of Minnesota Press, 1975), 344–69.

3. An exception to this generalization is Thomas Scanlon, "A Theory of Freedom of Expression," *Philosophy and Public Affairs* 2 (Winter, 1972): 199–216. His view in many ways is compatible with my own on the respective responsibilities of speakers and audiences in noncoercive communication situations.

4. Greenawalt, *Speech*.

5. Greenawalt, *Speech*, 58.

6. Greenawalt, *Speech*, 57.

7. Greenawalt, *Speech*, 59–60, 63–65.

8. Greenawalt, *Speech*, 65–66.

9. James G. Harbord, *The American Army in France* (Boston: Little, Brown and Co., 1936), 259.

10. Austin, "Performative Utterances," 239–40.

11. Searle, "Taxonomy," 349.

12. Searle, "Taxonomy," 349.

13. Greenawalt, *Speech*, 66–68.

14. The point being made here is essentially the same as that advanced by C. Edwin Baker who maintains that "the respect-for-autonomy rationale for protecting speech does not apply if the speaker coerces the other. . . . Speech behavior is normally noncoercive. Speech typically depends for its power on . . . the voluntary acceptance of listeners. Nonetheless, some speech can be coercive. But identification of coercive categories of speech requires great care. . . . In general, a person coercively influences another if (1) she restricts the other to options that are worse than the other had a moral or legitimate right to expect or (2) she employs means that she had no right to use for changing the threatened person's options" (*Human Liberty*, 56–60).

15. *U.S. v. O'Brien*, 391 U.S. 367 (1968) at 376.

16. *Young v. New York City Transit Authority*, 729 F.Supp. 341 (S.D.N.Y. 1990).

17. *Young v. New York City Transit Authority*, 903 F.2d 146 (2d Cir. 1990).

18. *Young*, 903 F.2d at 153.

19. *Young*, 903 F.2d at 156.

20. *Young*, 903 F.2d at 164.

21. *Young*, 903 F.2d at 159.

3. Fighting Words and Incitement

1. Supreme Court Justice Byron White may have been reflecting this view when he expressed the opinion that "fighting words are not a means of exchanging views, rallying supporters, or registering a protest; they are directed against individuals to provoke violence or to inflict injury" (*R.A.V. v. St. Paul*, 112 S. Ct. 2538 [1992] at 2553).

2. *Brandenburg v. Ohio*, 395 U.S. 444 (1969) at 447.

3. *Gooding v. Wilson*, 405 U.S. 518 (1972) at 524.

4. *Schenck v. U.S.*, 249 U.S. 47 (1919) at 52.

5. For example, *Abrams v. U.S.*, 250 U.S. 616 (1919); *Gitlow v. New York*, 268 U.S. 652 (1925); *Dennis v. U.S.*, 341 U.S. 494 (1951).

6. *Yates v. U.S.*, 354 U.S. 298 (1957) at 325; *Noto v. U.S.*, 367 U.S. 290 (1961).

7. This point of view was reasserted as recently as 1992 by Supreme Court Justice Antonin Scalia, writing for a majority of the Court in *R.A.V. v. St. Paul* as follows: "We have sometimes said that these categories of expression are 'not within the area of constitutionally protected speech' . . . or that the 'protection of the First Amendment does not extend' to them. . . . Such statements must be taken in context, however, and are no more literally true than is the occasionally repeated shorthand characterizing obscenity as 'not being speech at all.' . . . What they mean is that these areas of speech can, consistently with the First Amendment, be regulated *because of their constitutionally proscribable content* (obscenity, defamation, etc.) not that they are categories of speech entirely invisible to the Consitution" (*R.A.V. v. St. Paul*, 112 S. Ct. at 2553).

8. *Masses Publishing Company v. Patten*, 244 F. Supp. 535 (S.D.N.Y. 1917) at 540.

9. For a fuller explication of this point, see William E. Bailey, "The Supreme Court and Communication Theory: Contrasting Models of Speech Efficacy," *Free Speech Yearbook* 19 (1980): 1–15.

10. *Masses Publishing Company v. Patten*, 246 F.2d 24 (2d Cir. 1917) at 38.

11. For a fuller discussion of this process, see George Lakoff and Mark Johnson, *Metaphors We Live By* (Chicago: University of Chicago Press, 1980).

12. A more extensive treatment of the use of *fire* and other metaphors in the First Amendment opinions of the Supreme Court is provided in Diana C. Woods, "Communication Metaphors and the First Amendment: Fire and Water in Supreme Court Opinions" (Ph.D. diss., Northwestern University, 1991).

13. *Schenck v. U.S.*, 249 U.S. 247 (1919) at 252.

14. *Gitlow v. New York*, 268 U.S. 652 (1925) at 669.

15. *Dennis v. U.S.*, 341 U.S. 494 (1951) at 511.

16. *Frohwerk v. U.S.*, 249 U.S. 204 (1919) at 209.

17. *Abrams v. U.S.*, 250 U.S. 616 (1919) at 620.

4. Hate Speech

1. The *New York Times* reports that "all but four states now have some form of statute dealing with hate crimes, or 'bias-motivated' acts,

most of them passed in the 1980s. Most start with crimes already on the books, like trespass or assault, and add stiffer penalties if the crime was motivated by hate or bias" ("Hate-Crime Law Is Focus of Case on Free Speech," 1 Dec. 1991, 1).

2. The Hate Crimes Statistics Act, P. L. 101–275, 28 U.S.C. 534 (1990).

3. Lawrence, "Racist Speech," 452, 461.

4. See William L. Prosser, "Intentional Infliction of Mental Suffering: A New Tort," *Michigan Law Review* 37 (1939): 879, and "Insult and Outrage," *California Law Review* 44 (1956): 40.

5. Prosser, "Mental Suffering," 882–83.

6. *Johnson v. Sampson*, 208 N.W. 814 (Minn. 1926).

7. *Hustler v. Falwell*, 485 U.S. 46 (1988) at 53, 55.

8. *Public General Acts and Measures of 1965* Pt. II, Ch. 73 (London: Her Majesty's Stationery Office, 1966): 1619.

9. *Whitney v. California*, 274 U.S. 357 (1927) at 377.

5. Hate Crimes

1. *Wisconsin v. Mitchell*, No. 92–515. A Supreme Court decision was handed down on 11 June 1993, as this book was in press. The Court unanimously came to the same conclusions as does this chapter but without addressing some of the complexities and reservations discussed here.

2. *People v. Justice*, No. 1–90–1793 (Mich. Dist. Ct. 1990) at 6.

3. *People v. Justice*, No. 1–90–1793 at 6, 8.

4. *Dawson v. Delaware*, 117 L.Ed.2d 309 (1992).

5. *Dawson*, 117 L.Ed.2d at 317.

6. *Dawson*, 117 L.Ed.2d at 321.

7. *R.A.V. v. St. Paul.* 112 S. Ct. 2538 (1992) at 2538.

8. *R.A.V. v. St. Paul*, 464 N.W. 2d 507 (1991) at 511.

9. Brief *Amicus Curiae* of the American Civil Liberties Union, Minnesota Civil Liberties Union, and American Jewish Congress, In Support of Petitioner in *R.A.V. v. City of St. Paul, Minnesota*, 16.

10. *R.A.V. v. St. Paul*, 112 S. Ct. at 2538.

11. *R.A.V. v. St. Paul*, 112 S. Ct. at 2543–2547.

12. *R.A.V. v. St. Paul*, 112 S. Ct. at 2550, 2560.

13. *R.A.V. v. St. Paul*, 112 S. Ct. at 2553–2554.

14. *R.A.V. v. St. Paul*, 112 S. Ct. at 2561.

15. *R.A.V. v. St. Paul*, 112 S. Ct. at 2561.

16. Susan Gellman, "Sticks and Stones Can Put You in Jail, but Can Words Increase Your Sentence?" *UCLA Law Review* 39 (1991): 333–96.

17. Gellman, "Increase Your Sentence," 357.

18. Gellman, "Increase Your Sentence," 355–56.
19. Gellman, "Increase Your Sentence," 357.
20. Gellman, "Increase Your Sentence," 357.
21. Gellman, "Increase Your Sentence," 362.
22. California Penal Code, Title 11.6 ("Civil Rights"), Sec. 422.6 (c).
23. Gellman, "Increase Your Sentence," 367–68.
24. This is virtually the same conclusion as that reached by Martin Margulies, "Intent, Motive, and the R.A.V. Decision," *Criminal Justice Ethics* 11 (1992): 42–46. Although Margulies has serious doubts about the wisdom of enhanced penalties for hate crimes, he concedes that such statutes, if carefully drafted, can pass constitutional muster. The major concern expressed by Margulies, which is also among those raised by Gellman, is that the criminal law does not and should not delve into the motivations for a criminal act but only into the accused's *intent* in commiting that act. This distinction is a subtle one resting essentially on the difference between the most proximate purpose of a defendant's action—a purpose which society has decided must be criminalized— and the more ultimate purposes or motives the accused may have sought to achieve. But, as Margulies convincingly argues, statutes that enhance penalties for hate crimes must respect this distinction if they are to protect to the greatest extent possible the First Amendment right of defendants to believe and say what they wish. Offenders should be punished more severely than others for their criminal conduct only if they have intentionally selected their victims on the basis of the race, religion, ethnicity, or sexual orientation of those victims.

6. Sexist Speech

1. Jane Gross, "Schools Are Newest Arena for Sex-Harassment Cases," *New York Times*, 11 March 1992, A 1, A 18.
2. *Miller v. California*, 413 U.S. 15 (1973) at 24.
3. *Paris Adult Theatre v. Slaton*, 413 U.S. 49 (1973) at 58.
4. *State v. Henry*, 732 P.2d 9 (Or. 1987).
5. Schauer, *Free Speech*, 181.
6. Alain Robbe-Grillet, "For a Voluptuous Tomorrow," trans. Richard Howard, *Saturday Review*, 20 May 1972, 46.
7. *American Booksellers Association v. Hudnut*, 771 F.2d 323 (7th Cir. 1985); summarily affirmed, *Hudnut v. American Booksellers Association*, 475 U.S. 1001 (1986).
8. "Canada Court Says Pornography Harms Women and Can Be Barred," *New York Times*, 28 Feb. 1992, A 1.
9. "Canada Court," B 10.
10. Katrina Foley and Shiela Moreland, "The Dirty Secret—Frater-

nity Drinking Songs—Sexual Harassment," *Los Angeles Times*, 15 March 1992, M 6.

11. Clarence Page, "Pinups Today, Press Tomorrow? It's not a Pretty Picture," *Chicago Tribune*, 6 Nov. 1991, 19.

12. *Robinson v. Jacksonville Shipyards*, 760 F. Supp. 1486 (M.D. Fla. 1991).

13. *Jacksonville Shipyards*, 760 F. Supp. at 1542–43.

14. "Stroh's Case Pits Feminists Against ACLU," *Wall Street Journal*, 14 Nov. 1991, B 6.

15. "Stroh's Case," B 6.

16. A legal philosophy which buttresses and justifies this approach to the verbal harassment issue is persuasively described by Burt Neuborne, "Ghosts in the Attic: Idealized Pluralism, Community and Hate Speech," *Harvard Civil Liberties Civil Rights Law Review* 27 (1992): 371–406.

7. Information and Communication Theft

1. *Sidis v. F-R Publishing Co.*, 113 F.2d 806 (2d Cir. 1940) at 809. This phrase, enunciated by the U.S. Circuit Court of Appeals for the Second Circuit in an important case of the public disclosure of embarrassing private facts, was later quoted with apparent approval by the Supreme Court in a footnote to a decision involving a different sort of alleged invasion of privacy, i.e., casting the subject of the communication in a false light (*Time v. Hill*, 385 U.S. 376 [1967]).

2. E. L. Godkin, "The Rights of the Citizen—IV: To His Own Reputation," *Scribner's* 8 (July, 1890), 58–67.

3. Samuel D. Warren and Louis D. Brandeis, "The Right to Privacy," *Harvard Law Review* 4 (1890): 193–220.

4. John H. F. Shattuck, *Rights of Privacy* (Skokie, IL: National Textbook Co., 1977), 145.

5. "Les 100 Francais les plus riches," *Le Nouvel Observateur*, 16/22 Oct. 1987, 51–75.

6. William L. Prosser, "Privacy," *California Law Review* 48 (1960): 397.

7. An early and significant precedent to this effect was the case of *Sidis v. F-R Publishing Company*, 113 F 2d. 806.

8. *New York Times v. NASA*, 920 F.2d 1001 (D.C. Cir. 1990); *New York Times v. NASA*, 782 F. Supp. 628 (D.D.C. 1991). It is an indication of the closeness of this question that when the federal district court judge's initial ruling in favor of the *New York Times* was overturned by the full U.S. Circuit Court of Appeals for the District of Columbia and sent back to the district court for rehearing, it was by a vote of 6 to 5. The district court then reversed itself and ruled in NASA's favor.

9. Franklyn S. Haiman, *Speech and Law in a Free Society* (Chicago: University of Chicago Press, 1981), 86.

10. Rodney Smolla, *Free Speech in an Open Society* (New York: Alfred A. Knopf, 1992).

11. Smolla, *Free Speech*, 48–49.

12. William Prosser, *Handbook of the Law of Torts*, 3d ed. (St. Paul, MN: West Publishing Co., 1964), 699–700.

8. Victimless Communicative Actions

1. *O'Brien*, 391 U.S. at 376.

2. *Clark v. Community for Creative Non-Violence*, 468 U.S. 288 (1984) at 301.

3. *Community for Creative Non-Violence v. Watt*, 703 F.2d 586 (D.C.Cir. 1983).

4. *Clark*, 468 U.S. at 288.

5. *Clark*, 468 U.S. at 301.

6. *Clark*, 486 U.S. at 312.

7. *Employment Division, Oregon Department of Human Resources v. Smith*, 110 S. Ct. 1595 (1990).

8. *Barnes v. Glen Theatre*, 111 S. Ct. 2456 (1991).

9. *Employment Division*, 110 S. Ct. at 1606–15.

10. *Barnes*, 111 S. Ct. at 2456.

11. *Barnes*, 111 S. Ct. at 2458–63.

12. *Barnes*, 111 S. Ct. at 2468–71.

13. Justice Souter's point on this matter is supported by a 1989 decision of the Supreme Court in which a claim that dancing in a nonperformance context is a form of "association" protected by the First Amendment was rejected by the Court (*City of Dallas v. Stanglin*, 490 U.S. 19 [1989]).

14. *Barnes*, 111 S. Ct. at 2471–76.

15. *Barnes*, 111 S. Ct. at 2463–68.

16. Another eccentric example of the kind of majority decision-making Justice Scalia would find acceptable is provided in his opinion in *R.A.V. v. St. Paul* when he writes that "we cannot think of any First Amendment interest that would stand in the way of a State's prohibiting only those obscene motion pictures with blue-eyed actresses" (*R.A.V.*, 112 S. Ct. at 2547). In addition to illustrating his undiluted majoritarianism with respect to the regulation of nonsymbolic behavior, which he *thinks* he is referring to with this example, the comment demonstrates the ease with which he, like so many others, confounds action with speech and thus opens the door to social control of the latter as well as the former. For a ban on the exhibition of movies with blue-eyed ac-

tresses could only be based on an assumption that the *message communi-cated* to an audience, nonverbally and perhaps subliminally, by blue eyes is somehow different from, and more dangerous than, that communicated by brown or hazel-colored eyes. Hence, it is really speech, not action, that would be curbed in this instance of majority rule.

17. *Rider v. Board of Education of Independent School District*, 414 U.S. 1097 (1973).

18. *Clark*, 468 U.S. at 307, citing *Wisconsin v. Yoder*, 406 U.S. 205 (1972).

9. Morality and the Law

1. Lawrence Solum, "Freedom of Communicative Action: A Theory of the First Amendment Freedom of Speech," *Northwestern University Law Review* 83 (1988/89): 54–135.

2. Jurgen Habermas, *The Theory of Communicative Action*, trans. Thomas McCarthy, 2 vols. (Boston: Beacon Press, 1984).

3. Solum, "Communicative Action," 108.

4. *U.S. Postal Service v. Council of Greenburgh Civic Associations*, 453 U.S. 114 (1981).

5. *Greenburgh*, 453 at 155.

Index

Franklyn S. Haiman is John Evans Professor Emeritus of Communication Studies at Northwestern University and a vice-president of the American Civil Liberties Union. He is the author of numerous articles and books on freedom of speech. His 1981 volume *Speech and Law in a Free Society* received the American Bar Association's Silver Gavel Award and the Speech Communication Association's award for most outstanding scholarly book of the year.

Professor Haiman has been a Fulbright Visiting Lecturer in Communication Law at the University of Paris, a visiting scholar in Denmark and Japan, and a guest lecturer on scores of American campuses, including the A. Craig Baird Distinguished Professorship at the University of Iowa, the Silha Lectureship at the University of Minnesota, and the College of Communication Distinguished Lecturer at the University of Texas. He retired from Northwestern in 1991 after forty-three years on that faculty, eleven of them as chair of the Department of Communication Studies. Since then he has spent semesters as a visiting professor at the University of New Mexico, San Francisco State University, and the Annenberg School for Communication of the University of Pennsylvania.